WALL OF FIRE

WALL OF FIRE

A Diary of the Third Korean Winter Campaign

Dudley J. Hughes

HELLGATE PRESS
Central Point, Oregon

Library of Congress Cataloging-in-Publication Data
Hughes, Dudley J.
    Wall of fire : a diary of the third Korean winter campaign /
Dudley J. Hughes.
      p. cm.
    Includes bibliographical references.
    ISBN 1-55571-637-7
    1. Korean War, 1950–1953—Personal narratives, American.
    2. Hughes, Dudley J.—Diaries. 3. United States. Army—Diaries.
    I. Title.
    DS921.6.H885 2003
    951.904´28—dc22   2003016278

Designed by Jeff Wincapaw
Copyedited by Mary Ribesky and Marie Weiler
Proofread by Sharon Vonasch
Maps by Alvin Byrd
Photo separations by iocolor, Seattle
Produced by Marquand Books, Inc., Seattle
   www.marquand.com
Printed by Thomson-Shore, Inc., United States of America

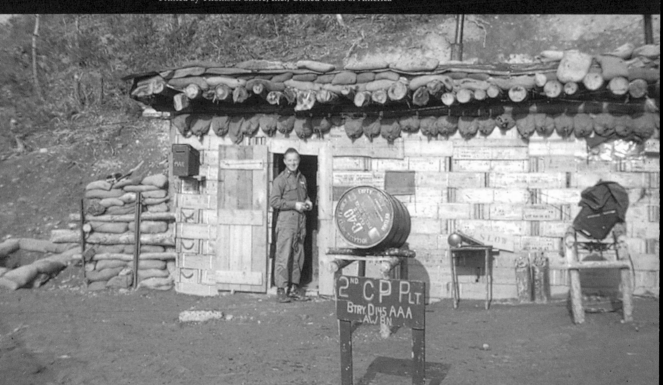

Contents

Illustrations

Maps

Figures

Preface

This is a true story, a diary, of a twenty-two-year-old, newly married second lieutenant who served in the Korean War during its last winter of combat. He was assigned a role in helping to defend the United Nations' heavily entrenched fortifications along the eastern Korean front. He and his twin brother served in adjacent units, directing massed fire from antiaircraft quad-50 machine guns against enemy ground troops. Techniques were developed that made possible accurate nighttime massed fire from the weapons, which had devastating effects on the enemy infantry. From a military historical viewpoint, much of this information has never before been published.

Memorandum after Cease Fire, Office of Chief of Military History

It was as an adjunct of infantry fighting that AAA (Army Antiaircraft Artillery) had its most decisive impact upon Eighth Army operations.

This was particularly true of the quad-50 (M-16), which had greater tactical flexibility in ground fighting and a visibly greater demoralizing effect upon the enemy infantry. . . . It would be difficult to exaggerate the effectiveness of the quad-50 when used in this role. Based on the Korean record, it can be said that, except for the accurate laying on of an air strike employing napalm and rockets, no other weapon available for the support of infantry depressed enemy firepower more quickly and fully, and in general discouraged the enemy from taking effective action. . . .

In Korea, the record of AA operations in close support of infantry was one of steady progress and rapid evolution. . . . All in all, it seems safe to conclude that support from the AA mounts was one of the chief sources of stiffening to the infantry line in Korea. (Office of Chief of Military History, 1963, 1)

WALL OF FIRE

Introduction

My generation grew up with war. When the Japanese attacked Pearl Harbor on 7 December 1941, I was twelve years old and still in grammar school. For the next five years Americans were united in an all-out war effort. Most of the young men were in uniform. Hollywood turned out films stirring a universal patriotic mood to new heights. At home, shortages of almost everything developed—food, fuel, and tires were rationed. New cars were unobtainable for the duration of the war. The speed limit on highways was 40 mph to save fuel and rubber. Hitchhiking became respectable, and no one would pass up a man in uniform. Every town had "scrap metal drives." As Boy Scouts, we would collect tin cans, pans, toys, and other scrap metal laid out in front of each household and create a huge pile along a rail siding to be shipped to a "war plant."

Early in the military buildup, people would line the streets and cheer when convoys of trucks carrying soldiers passed through our little town of Palestine in East Texas. The soldiers would throw small brass shell cases with a note inside giving their name and address to girls in the crowd. Later these convoys became commonplace and attracted less attention.

Actually, we lived about a mile from town. My father supervised the maintenance of a network of natural-gas pipelines for United Gas Company through several East Texas counties. We lived in a "company house" in a fenced-in compound that also held his office, tool houses, pipe racks, trucks, and car garages. A gang of men worked from there each day to troubleshoot any problems with the pipelines. They were mostly older workers, as the younger ones had been drafted.

My father had worked for United Gas since the company's beginning. As the company expanded, we lived in a number of towns in Louisiana, Mississippi, and Texas.

I have an identical twin brother, Dan. When we were born, in 1929, my parents were living in a company house in the Monroe Gas Field in Louisiana. This was the same year that the stock market crashed, initiating the Great Depression. Twin sisters were born five years later. My father was quite proud of two sets of twins. The laundrywoman said, "My, my—fo' in two whacks." Dan and Dudley were family names from previous twins. In fact, my father and his twin brother were named Dan and Dudley, respectively. From our family roots in Georgia, there were Dan and Dudley twins in the family as far back as the 1850s.

We moved to Palestine, Texas, in 1936. This was to be our place of longest residence, and it was here that we attended grammar school and high school. Our company house was in the Swanson Hill grammar-school district. This was a typical country school for the 1930s—a wooden three-room building with three teachers, one for each room. One room held the first through third grades, the second room the fourth through sixth grades, and the third the seventh and eighth grades. Toilets were outdoor privies. In winter, heat was furnished by a large woodburning furnace. Boys carried in wood during recess. In summer, the only air conditioning was open windows. A school bus carried us to and from school over several miles of dirt roads.

Dan and I, being twins, were constant companions growing up and occasionally settled disputes by fighting (which usually ended in a draw). As youngsters, we each had our own dog. When we fought, the dogs tore into each other to show their loyalty. In school fights, though, we were on the same side.

Living in the company compound gave us access to all sorts of tools and raw materials. We were always building and designing things, such as tree houses, boats, pipe cannons, and even a crude 14-foot Ferris wheel, popular with the Boy Scouts. Behind the compound we hunted and fished in the surrounding woods and creeks.

After grammar school, we went to Palestine High School in town. This was 1943, and World War II was already well underway. Coming from Swanson Hill, we were country hicks among the suave city students, but we soon merged into the group. I was very good at math and reading but never learned to spell worth a darn—blame it on Swanson Hill. For the first time, girls became more important than hunting and fishing. Three years later we graduated (high school lasted only three years at that time). A number of the male students dropped out of high school to volunteer for military service each year we were there.

A Taste of the Military

In 1946, my senior year of high school, World War II ended. Soon after this defeat of Germany and Japan, most of the men making up the US armed forces were released from active duty. But already, a new evil force threatened the world's short-lived peace. Communism, spreading from Russia, began to divide the globe into two camps. Most of the returning war veterans thought that we would eventually have to fight Russia, too.

After graduating from high school, I worked during summer vacation with the United Gas gang in Palestine, while Dan worked in Oklahoma on a Magnolia Petroleum Company oil-field crew. With Russia's aggressiveness, everyone felt that young men would soon be required to serve a tour in the military. I jumped the gun by joining the Texas National Guard's 36th Infantry Division and attended weekly meetings. My first real introduction into the military was a two-week summer camp at Fort Hood.

One of the most difficult adjustments one must make in the transition from civilian life to the military is the loss of privacy. At Fort Hood my unit was assigned to barracks with rows of double bunks in one long, open room. All of our belongings had to be stowed in a trunk at the aisle end of our bunk and in a small closet at its head. The barracks housed sixty or more men with double bunks only a few feet apart. Everyone was required to be in his bed by 2200 hours (10:00 PM), when lights were turned out. You learned to sleep in spite of the snoring, farting, squeaking beds, and movements of others.

At one end of the barracks was the latrine, a large open room with a row of some fifteen commodes, standing naked and only three feet apart, along one wall. A similar row of washbasins with mirrors against the opposite wall and a long trough, capable of accommodating a good number of men simultaneously, provided the urinal against an end wall. The shower was a large, open room behind the other wall with rows of showerheads for communal bathing. Any shyness one had on entering the military soon disappeared. As the sergeant in charge said, "We're going to sleep together, shave together, shit together, and shower together. After training we're going to fight together."

I had my first taste of beer at Fort Hood. Some of my roommates had more than just a taste of the brew. I woke up one night feeling that I was being rained on. One of the young guardsmen thought he was in the latrine and was pissing in my bunk. Was I mad! I jumped out of bed, grabbed him by the front of his uniform, dragged him down the aisle to the latrine, pushed him into the shower, turned on the cold water, and held him there until he partially sobered up. Then I dragged him back and made him change my sheets. We learned to fight our own fights and not go crying to the sergeant or the commanding officer.

Texas A&M

In 1946 my father was transferred to Dallas, where we moved into a larger United Gas camp with several company houses. He was district foreman for all of United Gas Company's East Texas pipeline system.

Dan and I enrolled in a junior college in Arlington, which was a branch school of Texas A&M, North Texas Agricultural College (NTAC). All of the colleges were flooded with returning veterans on the GI Bill. NTAC required ROTC (Reserve Officers' Training Corps) for all male students who had not already been in the service. We wore uniforms full-time on campus, but were allowed to commute daily to our home in Dallas.

After one and one-half years at NTAC, Dan and I were admitted to Texas A&M College at the close of 1948. At that time Texas A&M was an all-male, all-military college. Students were automatically enrolled in ROTC programs, which made them exempt from the draft. Also, I was released from the National Guard. All branches of the army were represented at A&M, as was the air force.

A massive snowstorm forced us to take a passenger train to College Station to begin the semester. Even though Dan and I had transferred from NTAC at sophomore level in studies, the Corps tradition called for all cadets to serve one semester as freshmen. This presented a particular problem, since all freshmen had been moved off campus to an abandoned army airfield several miles away. Only freshman classes were taught there. The purpose of this was to stop hazing, which had reached a brutal level over the college's long military history.

Sophomore and higher classes were taught on the main campus. We were assigned to B Battery Engineer Company on the main campus. Spartan, four-story (battalion size) dormitories were designed to house one military company, or battery, of sixty men on each floor. The dorms were built of brick, concrete, glass, and metal. No wood. No carpets. There was a washbasin with running water and mirror in each room. But there was only one latrine for each floor, which had an army-style open row of commodes, urinals, and a communal shower room. There were only four "pseudo" freshmen in the entire dormitory. We were all assigned to Company B on the third floor.

We were innocents entering the gates of hell. In Company B there were about eight seniors and sixteen juniors but thirty-two sophomores. Normally, there would be more freshmen than sophomores. In the chain of command, the seniors controlled the juniors, the juniors disciplined the sophomores, who in turn hazed the freshmen. Seniors were all officers of various ranks, juniors were sergeants, sophomores were corporals, and freshmen were privates. The sophomores were mad because they had suffered their freshman year, and there was no one to pass it down to, that is, until we showed up. Now there were four freshmen for thirty-two sophomores to vent their anger on.

It started the first night. At each meal the entire Cadet Corps was assembled by companies or batteries and marched to the mess hall in step with the famous Texas A&M military marching band. When we ran out of the dorm to fall in for the march, we were immediately surrounded by sophomores. They stood us at attention, screaming in our faces, finding fault with our uniforms, cutting off buttons, scaring us out of our wits. We first thought this was a joke, which only made them angrier. It turned out that this would be reenacted at every meal for months, to the bitter end of the semester. The sophomores gleefully took turns harassing us. In the mess hall the freshmen were placed one to a table, surrounded by seniors, juniors, and sophomores. Freshmen had to sit at attention during the entire meal. Food was served first to seniors, next to juniors, and then to sophomores; what was left went to the freshmen.

In the dormitory, there were no locks on doors to the two-man rooms. We had to post our class schedule on the door and had to have a pass to leave the room at any other time. We could not leave the campus for the entire semester. In effect we were under house arrest. Sophomores could burst into our room, day or night, to harass us or inspect our room. We were called "frogs."

"Frog Hughes, my roommate farted. Git in here and smell it up!" We had to run into the room and breathe heavily while standing at attention and being constantly berated.

Traditionally, the seniors had used three-foot paddles to chastise underclassmen who screwed up. This had been outlawed in the effort to stop hazing but was still being practiced by the old-timers. The sophomores probably suffered this punishment more than we did.

Our only salvation came between seven and ten o'clock each evening, when freshmen were required to sit at their desks with open books, whether we studied or not. We looked forward to this, since the sophomores were not allowed to harass us during the study period. Also, we learned to study.

There were no telephones in the rooms. We were required to write a letter home at least once a week. Radios were allowed but not during the study period. One of our freshmen broke under the strain and dropped out of college. The upperclassmen moved in a triple bunk and put the remaining three of us in the same room. The intimidation only got worse, but with our father borrowing money against his insurance policy to help put us through college, Dan and I were determined to ride it out.

Each spring there were intramural sports contests between units. Having no boxers or wrestlers in our unit, we freshmen were required to represent the company in these sports. Dan and I chose to wrestle while our roommate chose to box. Dan and I came out pretty well, but our roommate got beat up so badly that he had to check into the hospital.

After four months of this, we were hardened but had developed a degree of pent-up rage against our tormentors. Then came our chance to get even. The sophomore dance was scheduled to take place just before the semester ended. The company commander informed us that traditionally the freshmen were allowed to harass the sophomores the day of the dance. We started by timidly pouring buckets of water on them from the hallway window, three stories above the outdoor entrance, as they returned from class. The enraged sophomore would rush madly up the stairs. We would intercept him and drag him into the shower to be further doused while he screamed at us. In our glee we seemed to have superhuman strength.

When the sophomores finally got off to the dance, we were like sharks in a feeding frenzy. We went into the room of our greatest heckler, pulled the bedding from his bunk, stopped up his washbasin, and turned on the water. The water began to spill over into the room. We shut the metal door and stuffed a towel under it. The room began to fill with water. By now we had thrown all caution to the wind. We repeated this in the other sophomore rooms.

Soon a river of water was running down the hallway and cascading like a miniature Niagara Falls down the stairwell. The two floors below began to get the water, then it poured out the doors to the outside. The campus police arrived, then the commandant (Regular Army). They couldn't believe that three freshmen could cause so much havoc in so short a time. Sophomores returning found their rooms afloat. The commandant confined the entire company to quarters to clean the mess up and called for an inspection at eight o'clock the next morning. The sophomores and freshmen worked all night, prodded on by the upperclassmen. We swept out water, mopped, and tried to dry the wet bedding. The next morning everything was back in order, and we passed inspection. Needless to say, we paid dearly for it: the hidden paddles came out.

Looking back, this seems very foolish, but everyone has a breaking point, and we had about reached ours. In the Old Corps, this would have been a routine occurrence, handled entirely by the senior students within the company. But with the modern move to cut out hazing, the Regular Army officers, assigned to train the Corps, involved themselves. Some were not Aggies (Texas A&M alumni). They suggested expulsion. Intervention by our seniors, in fact by the whole company, saved us from being expelled. Even the sophomore victims seemed to have a grudging admiration for the magnitude of our insurrection.

This incident influenced our future in the army, however, in that we were switched to the artillery. At the end of the semester, we had completed our first two years of ROTC. The army required that we sign a contract for two more years, after which time we would become commissioned officers in the reserves. Because of our escapade, Dan and I were not offered a contract by the engineers, but instead were offered one in the Coast Artillery, which was short of officers. We moved to their dormitory. (Coast Artillery was the traditional name, but the contract was with the newer Army Antiaircraft Artillery.) I have never regretted the switch to the artillery.

Dan and I began our next semester at A&M as juniors, skipping the despised sophomore year altogether. We were free to travel as we pleased. We kept a tight line on the sophomores and began to enjoy life again. Our senior year was even better. Our grades were very good, we concentrated on our selected profession—geology—and in November I met a beautiful girl, at church in Dallas, who was constantly on my mind.

The discipline and comradery of the Texas A&M Corps develops an esprit de corps similar to that of Marines. This follows you through life. Throughout my tour in the army and the business world afterward, I was always happy to meet another Aggie and was proud to be one.

By the summer of 1951, we had completed four years of ROTC, including a summer training camp at Fort Bliss, Texas. My tenure at Texas A&M ended with my graduation in June 1951 with a bachelor of science degree in geology and an Army Officers Commission in the Army Antiaircraft Artillery (AAA).

The Korean War began just four years after World War II ended and raged during my last year in college. I had missed WWII, but was in line for this war. Three months after being commissioned, orders came for me to report for active duty at Fort Bliss as a second lieutenant in the antiaircraft artillery.

Dan had also been commissioned at Texas A&M as a second lieutenant in the AAA and called to active duty at Fort Bliss. We spent the first few months there in Student Officers School, while heavy fighting was still under way in Korea.

Robbie

The easy schedule of the Officers School appeared to offer an ideal time for me to marry the beautiful girl from Dallas. Miss Robbie Lou Watson was a hazel-eyed blond who had been chosen one of six beauties of the Texas A&M Class of '51 Vanity Fair contest. Since A&M was an all-military boys' school, we had been courting long distance for over a year, primarily by my hitchhiking to Dallas almost every weekend. At the Aggie Ring Dance just before graduation, Robbie accepted my proposal. I was jubilant. Secretly, I was afraid that if I left her unattached while I served a tour of duty overseas, she might get tired of waiting.

Robbie made all the wedding arrangements—sending out invitations, lining up the church, planning the reception, and numerous other details. My brother was best man, several of my classmates served as groomsmen, and our sisters and Robbie's friends were bridesmaids. The army would grant me only a five-day leave (including a weekend) for the wedding, so we spent our one-night honeymoon in a Dallas hotel, then packed our new Plymouth with our wedding gifts and Robbie's clothes, and headed for El Paso, the home of Fort Bliss.

Fresh out of college, I was penniless. As a single second lieutenant, I had made $180 per month, and as a married second lieutenant, I would still only make about $230. The Plymouth cost $1,200, so Robbie made the initial payment from savings she had earned before we were married.

She said, "You're marrying me for the money."

"No honey, what I married you for, money couldn't buy." She smiled warmly.

We drove our Plymouth the 650 miles from Dallas to El Paso, spending one more memorable night along the route. After leaving Dallas and Fort Worth, the landscape became more arid, with scrubby brush and hundreds of oil wells. The air smelled faintly of sulfur and crude oil. Oil

Robbie Watson, one of six senior-class beauties, Texas A&M, Vanity Fair contest, 1951.

Dudley Hughes. Only seniors were allowed to wear boots. Texas A&M, 1951.

She said yes! Aggie Ring Dance, May 1951.

The wedding, 10 November 1951.

well flares dotted the night as far as the eye could see, like candles on a giant birthday cake. The smell was perfume to my nose—as my degree was in petroleum geology—but repugnant to Robbie, who did not share my enthusiasm for the smell of crude oil. In the early 1950s, the State of Texas produced about one-fourth of the world's crude oil (23.6 percent in 1951) and could be compared to the Saudi Arabia of today.

Eventually almost all signs of human habitation disappeared except for the narrow ribbon of two-lane highway that stretched out to the horizon ahead of us. The landscape became even more arid, with rolling sand dunes and little vegetation besides tumbleweeds, thorny shrubs, and cacti.

At El Paso we checked into the Alamo Motel. The luggage and wedding gifts filled the room. Dan soon arrived and dropped off more wedding gifts. We had to crawl over boxes to get to the bathroom. The next morning I donned my uniform and reported for duty, leaving Robbie in the overflowing room.

Robbie knew nothing about the military but nevertheless went to post command, where she had been told that we could apply for an apartment on the post through Sergeant Miller. She filled out the application and handed it to the person in charge. She asked, "Are you Sergeant Miller?"

"No young lady, I'm only a colonel."

"Well, please pass this application on to the sergeant when he comes in."

"Yes ma'm."

We moved into a small apartment on the post at 202C Collins Drive, which became our happy home for many months. She spent the next few weeks frugally shopping for furniture while I spent my days in Officers School.

Robbie learned that the post was offering free swimming lessons at the Fort Bliss outdoor pool for dependants of military personnel. Because of the threat of polio (then called "infantile paralysis") for children growing up in the 1930s and 1940s, swimming pools had been open only to adults in the summer, when the disease was most rampant. As a result, many young people, including Robbie, never learned to swim. I had learned to swim in winter at an indoor heated pool at the YMCA.

Robbie signed up for the swimming lessons. At the first lesson, she learned that the water was cold in spite of El Paso's 100-degree weather. Rapid evaporation in the arid climate kept the water cool. The instructors, who were mostly enlisted men, and expert swimmers, encouraged her to stick with it. "You'll get used to the cold," they said. After several lessons, I decided to drop by to see how she was doing. Robbie, in her swimsuit, was the center of the instructors' attention. Other students, mostly little kids, were struggling around in the water on their own while the instructors fawned over Robbie. She seemed oblivious to their attention and was trying hard to learn. I tactfully suggested that she was trying to swim with half her body out of the water and she must put her face in the water. She eventually dropped out of the class, much to the instructors' dismay. (Robbie never did become a proficient swimmer, even many years later when we had our own pool, but she had plenty of other "redeeming qualities.")

Fort Bliss Antiaircraft Artillery Training Battery

During World War II, the Army Antiaircraft Artillery and Field Artillery (FA) were separate branches of the US Army. Antiaircraft Artillery was originally derived from the Coast Artillery, but by the time the Korean War started, the AAA ("triple A") had become a branch of the FA. Fort Bliss was the AAA training center of the US Army. Soldiers were trained in the operation of large antiaircraft 90 mm cannons, which spotted the sky with the dreaded flak, like we see in World War II movies. Their purpose was to bring down high-flying bombers.

Less spectacular were training batteries of smaller, mobile automatic weapon (AAA AW) systems for shooting down low-flying planes. There were two principal antiaircraft automatic weapons. One was a turret mounted with four 50-caliber machine guns (quad-50s), and the other a 40 mm cannon. A quad-50 turret fastened to the bed of an armored halftrack vehicle made up a mobile weapon labeled the M-16. The four 50-caliber machine guns could be fired together, spewing out murderous streams of armor-piercing incendiary (API) bullets. Each 50-caliber round had a small phosphorus charge, which flashed when it struck. Every fifth round was a tracer. A single gunner inside the turret could swing the guns up and down or spin them around in any direction to follow targets. Two gunner's assistants carried ammunition to continually reload the guns and change hot barrels.

"Caliber" is the measure of the diameter of the bore of a gun. On large-bore guns it is measured in inches. On small bore guns it is measured in hundredths of an inch. Since the 50-caliber can be considered a small arm or a cannon, it is sometimes written as "caliber .50" and sometimes as "50-caliber." Either is probably correct as the bore is one-half inch. Most of the official reports in the Korean War use "caliber .50," but this account will use the term "50-caliber," as that term was more commonly used after Korea. In the modern military, gun bores are seldom measured in caliber.

The second weapon of the mobile arsenal was the 40 mm automatic cannon. It could be rapidly maneuvered by two people operating hand cranks to follow enemy planes. Other crew were necessary to load and fire the gun. All of the training emphasized methods to destroy low-flying aircraft by manual sighting from the ground.

On graduating from Officers School in January 1952, I was assigned as a platoon officer to the cadre of B Battery, 4th Training Battalion, AAA AW. Each of the training batteries had cadres made up of several officers and noncommissioned personnel who trained new troops (cadres were the permanent instructors in the training batteries). In addition to weapons training, we led marches through the desert, sometimes in burning heat and other times in windy cold. We bivouacked in the desert, at times enduring blinding sandstorms or avoiding rattlesnakes. On the desert firing ranges, the recruits practiced firing live ammunition at targets towed by drones or small planes.

Even training had its casualties. During a sandstorm, a trainee 20 feet from me had his head bowed into the wind and sand and was run over by a towed 40 mm cannon, which crushed his pelvis. During the hot marches several recruits suffered heat strokes. Cadres had it better than trainees. I was able to go back to my small apartment and my beautiful wife as each day's training ended, except when on bivouac in the field or on night duty.

Every six weeks the entire battery was broken up, and 250 trainees were shipped out as replacements, mostly to Korea but some to Germany. (US forces were strong in Germany to discourage Russia from entering the Korean conflict.) A fresh group of trainees then moved into the battery huts, and the training program was repeated. During my duty at B Battery, we had trained and shipped out five groups by the end of July 1952. I sometimes wondered how many of them were later wounded or killed. Then my time came—I received orders to Korea.

Dan was in another similar training battery. He still led a carefree life in the Bachelor Officers' Quarters (BOQ) and made the nightclub circuits with other single officers. He received his overseas orders to Germany, a single man's dream. He had a big laugh over my bad luck. Then we remembered—twins could request to serve together. At headquarters, I requested to serve with Dan in Germany. The warrant officer in charge said, "No problem. Both of you turn in your orders, and we'll ship you out together." He kept his word. We both received orders to Korea. Dan took the change pretty well, except to remind me of it periodically over the next fifty years.

My battery commander at Fort Bliss was Capt. Avery Peoples, who had been commissioned from the ranks while serving in World War II and then made a career of the army. When the Korean War started, he was rushed to that battleground in the early stages of fighting. He remained in combat for over a year during the hectic mobile phase of the war. Avery had earned nine battle stars from different campaigns in the two wars. Only a handful of the military ever matched that record. He presented me with a German Luger that he had captured in World War II and carried in Korea. After my tour in Korea, I returned the Luger to him.

The Korean War Before I Arrived, 1950–52

Time has largely erased from people's minds the magnitude of the Communist threat, which engulfed the world immediately after World War II. As soon as Germany surrendered in 1945, Russia began to install Communist governments in captured eastern satellite countries and in East Germany. Later Stalin tried to force the Allies out of West Berlin.

More pertinent to Korea, Mao Tse-tung's Communist forces waged a four-year civil war in China against Chiang Kai-shek's American-sponsored Nationalist armies. In 1949 the Communists took over all of mainland China, forming the People's Republic of 700 million Chinese. They maintained a huge army of 5 million seasoned troops.

It is hardly surprising that, after the success of the Chinese Communists, the North Koreans believed they could take South Korea with no interference from the United States. The last American troops had been withdrawn from South Korea by 29 June 1949. The Korean War began one year later, on 25 June 1950, with a surprise attack by superior North Korean Communist forces against South Korean military units. Both armies were positioned along the 38th Parallel, the arbitrary boundary between North and South Korea, chosen by the superpowers after World War II. The South Koreans had no tanks, antitank weapons, or artillery heavier than 105 mm, and their air force consisted of only a few trainer-type aircraft. The attacking armies had 50 percent more troops, who were much better trained and equipped. Their weapons included armor, modern jet fighters, and ground-attack bombers. The only Americans still in South Korea were the Korean Military Advisory Group (KMAG), who were few in number and not equipped for combat.

The South Korean forces were quickly routed, and the invaders swept down the peninsula with little resistance. The first new American combat troops arrived 1 July 1950, followed soon after by a British brigade. These were the beginning of a United Nations (UN) force being assembled to protect South Korea. The early American troops were fresh from occupational duty in Japan and poorly suited for combat. Their light antitank weapons could not stop the Russian-made tanks. They suffered a series of quick defeats with many casualties, and many were taken prisoner. By 4 August, the defenders had been pushed back to a small perimeter around the city of Pusan, at the southernmost tip of the Korean Peninsula. Although it appeared they might be pushed into the Sea of Japan, fire from the navy's big guns helped hold the perimeter.

The situation remained desperate for several weeks while the UN continued to bring in reinforcements. Attempts to break out from the siege of Pusan had little success, even as the UN forces strengthened.

In what proved to be a stroke of brilliance, Gen. Douglas MacArthur secretly loaded an invasion force on troop ships. He then launched an amphibious landing at Inchon on 15 September 1950, less than three months after the fighting started. Although few of his peers condoned this action, it was possibly the greatest military feat of his career.

MacArthur's hastily assembled Tenth (X) Corps, spearheaded by the 1st and 5th Marines, stormed Inchon and pushed on to Seoul. The ferocity of their assault overwhelmed the North Korean defenders, who were soon in fast retreat. Many of the American troops were seeing their first combat, but some acts of bravery were outstanding.

First Lt. Henry A. Commiskey Sr. of Hattiesburg, Mississippi, was awarded the Medal of Honor for his part in action with the 1st Marine Division at Yongdungpo:

> Directed to attack hostile forces well dug in on Hill 85, 1st Lt. Commiskey, spearheaded the assault, charging up the steep slopes on the run. Coolly disregarding the heavy enemy machinegun and small arms fire, he plunged on well forward of the rest of his platoon and was the first man to reach the crest of the objective. Armed only with a pistol, he jumped into a hostile machinegun emplacement occupied by five enemy troops

and quickly disposed of four of the soldiers with his automatic pistol. Grappling with the fifth, 1st Lt. Commiskey knocked him to the ground and held him until he could obtain a weapon from another member of his platoon and killed the last of the enemy guncrew. Continuing his bold assault, he moved to the next emplacement, killed two more of the enemy and then led his platoon toward the rear nose of the hill to rout the remainder of the hostile troops and destroy them as they fled from their positions. (Medal of Honor Citation; see www.homeofheroes.com/moh/citations_1950_kc/commiskey_henry.html)

Tables were abruptly turned. The bulk of the North Korean troops were concentrated around the Pusan perimeter, leaving fewer defenders at Inchon and Seoul. These cities were quickly taken, and UN forces pressed eastward to disrupt Communist supply lines. A disorderly retreat of North Korean units from Pusan followed. UN troops attacked from Pusan, following the North Koreans northward. Large numbers of the enemy were trapped and taken prisoner. The remaining North Koreans retreated across the 38th Parallel, with UN forces in hot pursuit. The North Korean Peoples Army straggled northward in small groups as village after village fell to the UN troops.

UN prisoners being held by the Communists were hampering their retreat. Some were brutally killed with their hands tied behind their backs.

MacArthur divided his forces into two groups. On the west, the 8th Army advanced northward through the more heavily populated North Korean towns. On the east coast, the X Corps, with the marines and ROK (Republic of Korea) units, advanced north and inland from the coast. The 8th Army was separated from the X Corps by a rugged mountain range, with practically no roads to allow one group to assist the other. Dividing his forces proved to be a devastating mistake for MacArthur.

As UN forces approached the Yalu River (North Korea's border with China), Chinese forces attacked ROK troops on the eastern side of the peninsula on 25 October. During the next four days, the Chinese halted the 8th Army in the west and the X Corps in the northeast. For ten days the tide of the battle turned decisively in favor of the Chinese. Then suddenly they withdrew and disappeared. Their reason for breaking off the action was misinterpreted. MacArthur paused for only two weeks to regroup, then ordered a resumption of the drive to the north. This was the second costly miscalculation on the general's part, which would result in a major defeat for the UN forces. After the warning from the first attacks, some believed he should have dropped back and consolidated his forces in anticipation of a larger attack.

On 26 November, the Chinese forces launched their counterattack. While the American units were road-bound with heavy vehicles, tanks, and artillery, the Chinese were on foot, armed with light weapons, grenades, and recoilless rocket launchers. They were able to move through the mountains and set up roadblocks, then ambush the retreating UN forces in a gauntlet of fire from the mountainsides. In addition to enemy fire, the brutal arctic winter had set in with temperatures of 30 degrees below zero, strong winds, and snow. The American troops lacked proper clothing, boots, and sleeping bags. During the retreat southward, the UN troops suffered the greatest number of casualties of any period during the war, from both enemy action and weather. Many were captured.

The X Corps was engaged at the Chosin Reservoir and forced to retreat, under constant attack, to Hungnam, a port on the Sea of Japan. From there the survivors were evacuated by ships. The 8th Army faced a similar situation in the east, with men fleeing from the enemy and leaving wounded behind. A large number were forced to surrender. By Christmas Day, the Chinese troops had crossed the 38th Parallel into South Korea and retaken Seoul.

As new reinforcements arrived, the UN forces were able to gradually slow the Communist advance and actually stop it by mid-January. On 9 December 1950 the X Corps was incorporated into the 8th US Army of Korea (EUSAK), with two other corps. The UN troops initiated a counterattack, forcing the Communists to begin a retreat on all fronts by 13 March 1951. The Chinese attempted another offensive in April, which was halted. The ground was retaken by mid-May, and the fighting moved into the eastern sector of North Korea.

A decision was then made at the UN headquarters in New York that created a stalemate that still exists a half-century later. The push to the north was halted along a line that could be easily defended, near the 38th Parallel. Retreating North Korean and Chinese armies found that their pursuers were no longer at their heels. Snatched from almost certain defeat, they turned and regrouped. On 25 June 1951, one year after the war began, the Chinese radio asked for a cease-fire. Armistice negotiations began at Kaesong on 10 July, but these quickly faltered and were discontinued. Cease-fire discussions were resumed at Panmunjom in October 1951 and would continue off and on for most of the next two years.

Agreement on a demarcation line was reached on 27 November 1951. The armies faced each other along a natural defense line across the Korean peninsula. The eastern portion of the line began at the Sea of Japan just south of Kaesong, then followed the Nam River Valley southward to the Soyang River Valley, then westward north of Chorwon, then southwestward past Panmunjom to the Yellow Sea. The line was north of the 38th Parallel except the portion southwest of Panmunjom (see Map 1, p. 41).

Each side dug in with heavily fortified battlements of sandbagged bunkers connected by trenches, reminiscent of World War I. The fortifications became elaborate enough to withstand hours of pounding by artillery, bombs, and mortars with minimal casualties. The Americans had achieved complete air superiority. US jets engaged the Chinese Migs along the Yalu River (Mig Alley) and destroyed them with a kill ratio of ten to one. Flights of Saber jets continually patrolled immediately south of the Yalu River and engaged any enemy plane that crossed the river, usually with fatal results. Essentially no enemy planes approached the main line of resistance (MLR) during the last two years of the war.

In North Korea, no daytime troop movements, supply trains, or motor convoys could venture into the open without risk of destruction from the sky. Small artillery spotter planes (Cessna L-19 Birddogs) continually patrolled the Communist trench lines, calling in immediate fire on any movement within artillery range. To withstand the heavy bombing from the air, the North Koreans and Chinese dug a network of caves and tunnels in conjunction with their trench system. They stayed in these underground shelters during daylight hours.

A de facto cease-fire began in late 1951 and lasted until October 1952, during which period the casualty rate on both sides was low. The final ten months of the war saw a steady increase in action and casualties, while talks proceeded at Panmunjom. "In the spring of 1953 the Communists decided to use the battlefield to apply pressure upon the negotiations and to prepare some basis for their claim of military victory" (Hermes 1966, 508).

The UN army could move about freely south of the lines, out of sight of the enemy. Communist gunners blindly dropped rounds of mortar or artillery during daylight to harass their UN foes, but these bombardments were mostly ineffective. UN daylight fire against the Communists was more intense and more effective with help from the spotter planes. The close proximity of the opposing trench lines made daylight exposure to snipers too hazardous for movement in many of the trenches. During the mobile phase of the war, most of the fighting had taken place during the daytime, but trench warfare relegated the fighting to nighttime. Bombardments by both sides, utilizing artillery and mortar, continued nightly with surprising intensity, along with nightly probing attacks by patrols or larger units. The final stages of the war were fought along the stationary MLR with minimal exchange of real estate.

The Troops

The Korean War was the first "color blind" war to be fought by the US military. In World War I and World War II, combat was conducted by white troops except for marginal participation by selected "all black" units. In Korea, troops were integrated and shared combat equally. White troops served under black officers and noncommissioned officers (NCOs or non-coms). White and black fought together and died together. Combat is a great equalizer. Skin color fades when your life depends on the support of your comrades.

Another phenomenon, called "rotation," was developed during the Korean War. During World War I and World War II, military service was generally for the "duration" of the war, with the exception that the air force allowed rotation of bombing crews after approximately 35 missions. In Korea the troops who had been involved in the war during its first hectic months, when many were World War II "recalls" and casualties ran the highest, did not believe they should have to serve indefinitely as sentries in a stalemated war. This was especially compelling since there was a vast untapped pool of reserves and potential recruits in the United States.

A rotation system was put in place based on earned points. At the time I arrived, thirty-six points were required to complete a tour and return to the States. Frontline combat troops were awarded four points per month, requiring nine months in the combat zone to rotate. Between the regimental headquarters and front lines (plus or minus ten miles) was a three-point area. Rear echelon in Korea were awarded two points and duty in Japan one point. As a result, the frontline units were soon made up of replacements, and there was constant turnover throughout the remainder of the war. The comradery of units that had trained together was lacking, but surprisingly, the system worked quite well, and replacements upheld the honor of their units. Knowing you would rotate on a fixed schedule was a morale booster. It was this "pipeline system" that Dan and I entered in 1952.

Almost all accounts of the Korean War describe the first year of the war in great detail and devote 95 percent or more of their text to the battles, military activities, and political decisions before the establishment of the final line. The last two years of the war are barely mentioned. That is understandable in view of the high number of casualties, the suffering from severe cold, the high death rates in Communist prisoner-of-war (POW) camps, and the brave acts of many soldiers during the mobile phase of the war. It's true that the mobile phase was more rugged and its casualty rate much higher, but thousands of replacement soldiers were exposed to many months of stationary combat during the last two years. Most chronicles barely mention this longest period of the Korean War. Few people are aware that 50 percent of the UN Korean War casualties took place during the last two years of trench warfare. There were continuous artillery and mortar duels. Infantry patrols in no-man's-land held the same risk as the earlier fighting. Casualties came more from shrapnel and land mines than small-arms fire, as there was less face-to-face contact between individual soldiers.

This account will attempt to portray a true insight into this longest but mostly forgotten phase of the Korean War. It is an accurate description of my experiences during 1953, the final winter of combat, the Third Korean Winter Campaign.

The Leave

After being relieved from duty at Fort Bliss on 31 July 1952, Robbie and I began our move back to Dallas. We had the beginnings of home furnishings and the Plymouth sedan, all of which were on time payments. The government paid for the moving van that picked up our furniture. Once in Dallas we stored the furniture and moved in with Robbie's parents. After the discipline and grueling schedule at Fort Bliss, the seven weeks of leave languished at a lazier pace than I really wanted. Robbie and her mother thought I would suffer starvation in Korea and plied me with food. We visited old friends and loafed. I gained several pounds.

My father arranged for us to have a week alone on a private lake with a well-equipped cabin, set deep in the piney woods of East Texas. This would be our real honeymoon. We were overwhelmed by the beauty of the sparkling lake nestled between tall pines. There was a boat tied to the pier in front of the cabin. After unpacking, Robbie wanted to fish, so we paddled the boat to a likely spot. I rigged the lines and baited her hook. She had a fish before I had a line in the water. I took it off the hook and rebaited her line. Again she pulled in a fish. This went on for some time, while she did all the fishing and I did all the work. It was fun to see how excited she was, and we soon had an ice chest full of fish. I wanted to go in but she didn't. "You will have to bait your own hook and take your fish off if we are going to keep on fishing," I said. She agreed and made a face as she baited her hook. By dark we had enough fish to feed a squad. I spent the next two hours dressing the fish and putting them in the freezer. By the time we cooked dinner and tried to bathe off the fish smell, it was too late for much honeymooning.

At dawn the next morning she woke me up wanting to fish again. Again it was an all-day fishing affair with more fish to clean. This went on again on the third day. By then I had realized that Robbie had an unquenchable appetite for fishing. The food rationing of World War II was too fresh in our minds to throw any fish back, so I spent most of the evenings cleaning fish. The crowning blow was discovery of the trot line strung between two stumps in the water. She had never seen one. I explained that it was baited at night, mainly to catch catfish. Of course, she wanted to try her hand at it. Somewhat reluctantly I baited it right at dark. After dinner we went to bed exhausted from the day's fishing. About midnight she woke me up to run the trot line. I explained that the fish would still be there in the morning, but she wanted to go then, so we did. Sure enough, we had several respectable catfish. The rest of the week we fished both day and night. The freezer overflowed. I became very grouchy—so much for the honeymoon. Robbie has never tired of fishing, even to this day.

En Route to the Far East

At the end of October this pleasant interlude ended. I had received orders to report to Fort Lawton, in Seattle, Washington, not later than 2 November 1952, where I was scheduled to leave by ship for Japan.

From the day I left until I returned from Korea, I wrote Robbie a letter almost every day. Most of each letter contained personal communication between husband and wife, but these letters also gave a day-to-day account of activities, of course minimizing the danger from combat. Fifty years later, as I began to write this journal, she presented me with the entire set of about 150 letters, still intact. When she asked, "Where are the letters I wrote to you?" after a short, pained silence, I quipped, "Would you believe the Communists captured them?" "No," she replied. "I didn't think you would."

Robbie's letters, along with other information at my disposal, enabled me to recount this story, from the day I left until my return, in the form of a diary. The italicized extracts are from these letters.

1 November 1952

On November 1, Robbie and my father drove me to Love Field, in Dallas, to board a four-engine prop plane bound for Los Angeles (this was before commercial jets). They were trying to be brave, but Robbie was teary eyed and clung to me until I had to push her away. I boarded the plane without looking back. Through the window I saw them wave as the plane taxied away. I didn't really feel as brave as I was acting.

Flying time to Los Angeles was about six hours, not counting intermediate stops. At one stop they helped aboard a very young soldier, heavily bandaged, with one leg missing below the knee—a casualty fresh back from Korea. My stomach churned at the sight. I was still somewhat despondent when we landed in LA with a two-hour layover before taking another flight to Seattle.

Much to my surprise, one of my old geology professors, Fred Smith, now Colonel Smith, appeared on the plane and led me off. My brother, Dan, who had taken a flight the day before, was waiting outside with Fred's wife, Odette. Fred had been recalled to active duty and was now in charge of the replacement pipeline through LA. He had been one of the most well-liked professors at Texas A&M, and he tried to intercept as many of his former students coming through as possible. Dan had called Fred when he arrived and accepted his invitation to spend the night at his house. He was given a tour of the city.

For my two-hour layover, they took me on a hurried tour of Los Angeles, Hollywood, and most of the other interesting spots. (The city was much smaller then than it is today.) Then Dan rode on the same plane with me as far as San Francisco, as his orders were to ship out from there. Los Angeles had been an interesting place to visit except for the heavy smog, which made our eyes water when we ventured outdoors.

After only a few days' orientation in San Francisco, Dan was sent to Japan by commercial air service. He boarded a Constellation, a long-range "triple tailed," propellor-driven, four-engine aircraft used in overseas flights at that time. After eleven hours, the plane landed in Honolulu. Two hours later they took off and after another eleven hours of flying time landed at Wake Island. Eleven hours from there, they landed in Tokyo. Altogether, flying time was thirty-three hours.

Seattle, Washington

Continuing on after Dan left, I arrived in Seattle around eight o'clock, some three hours after dark. Not wanting to check into Fort Lawton that late, I checked into the New Washington Hotel, one of the major hotels in the city. Danny Kay was in the lobby of the hotel and greeted me with one of the short comic routines that he reserved for servicemen. Also that evening I had my first fresh salmon for dinner. Being from East Texas, I thought salmon came only in cans.

2 November 1952

My first letter to Robbie: *I've just signed in at Fort Lawton and now share a room with a couple of other 2nd lieutenants. This morning I looked over Seattle and the waterfront. It's strange to be in a heavy fog after "dry" Dallas. I've been amazed at the clear blue-green color of the Pacific. This country is really beautiful. . . . We're so near the Canadian border that Canadian money is circulated with the US currency. Change may be half Canadian and half US. [This was before currencies were floated.]*

3 November 1952

Well I may as well throw away my comb. I don't have any more use for it than your daddy does for a toothbrush. This is about the best crewcut I've ever had, though. . . .

I was issued some more heavy clothing, so I'm sending my extra clothes home. You should receive a box C.O.D. with my green blouse, pink pants [dress uniform], green bill cap, and field jacket, within the next few days. I drew $45 pay and found I would receive an extra $5 per day as long as I remained in port. . . . Today we were told that we would go by boat, leaving about the 11th.

Even with these wool uniforms, I was poorly dressed for the arctic temperatures I would encounter. My heaviest coat was a drab olive cotton topcoat with a thin flannel button-in lining.

4 November 1952

Well I've about finished being processed and probably won't have much to do except wait for the next few days. . . . The wind is from the north today and I'm getting rather cold in spite of my heavy wool clothing.

All of us being shipped out were herded into a very large theater for a series of lectures. Of course, one was on venereal disease with a film that was graphic enough to scare one into never again having sex. Another was on alcohol. The master sergeant making the presentation said, "If you don't drink, whatever you do, don't start now. That leaves more for us who do."

Today I drew travel pay amounting to $39. When I leave here I may have to send you a money order as we are allowed to carry only $50 cash overseas. . . .

Phil Mason . . . Dan's roommate at Fort Bliss . . . lives right across the hall from me. Tonight I think we'll watch the election returns on television at the officers' club."

The presidential race was to be decided between Dwight Eisenhower and Adlai Stevenson. On 4 November 1952, we sat at the bar in the Fort Lawton Officers' Club watching one of the early model black-and-white TV sets until Eisenhower was declared the winner. Everyone in the officers' club cheered. With the war going on, it was comforting to have a former general at the helm.

5 November 1952

There has been a change in my orders. . . . I'll leave here on the 7th and fly to Alaska.

I would then head on to Japan by way of the Aleutian Islands. The intent of this change was to move forward my time of arrival in Japan, but unforseen developments would slow this process.

7 November 1952

I didn't fly out today after all . . . , it may be Monday or later before I leave.

The delay occurred because the plane had developed engine trouble.

I had dinner in town last night . . . and bought some cold-weather clothes, about $20 worth. My days here are pretty monotonous. I sleep late, go to the club for coffee and donuts, then read magazines until noon. After lunch, which is usually quite good in the mess hall, I loaf around and read some. In the evenings I usually go to the club and watch television or go to the movie.

8 November 1952

The coming weekend looks sort of drab. Sure wish you were here so we could run up to Vancouver or some scenic spot for the weekend. I've never seen woods so vividly colored as these are. The huge fir trees furnish the background, while brightly colored aspen, poplar, birch, and many other types . . . punctuate the dark green with bright colors. There are hundreds of lakes and bays, all clear blue. On the west are the Olympic mountains. . . . To the east, the Cascade Range reaching above 14,000 feet. The weather is seldom clear enough to see them.

There are a good many guys coming back from FECOM [Far East Command] and Alaska.

11 November 1952

It wasn't until 11 November 1952 (one day after my first wedding anniversary), that the plane was ready. I boarded at McChord Air Force Base and took off for Japan, with the first intermediate stop to be Anchorage.

I'm writing this aboard a Canadian Air Force plane that is transporting us to Anchorage, Alaska. It's just a military plane with little web seats built along the walls, and a jumble of packs and straps in the center where baggage and miscellaneous equipment are stored. Officers are sprawled in about every conceivable position on the equipment, in the web seats, and in stretcher beds that are suspended from the roof. We've been flying for about five hours and are still about three hours out of Anchorage. We'll lay over for a couple of hours, then fly another eight hours to Shemya in the Aleutian Islands. There we will lay over fourteen hours, then on to Japan. Flying time alone will total thirty-three hours, and I'm already tired after five hours. (The boy across the aisle just puked all over himself.)

I won't be sending any money home . . . because I spent all except about $40. . . . There was a boy coming back [from Korea with a chrome-plated] 45 caliber pistol. . . . I bought it from him for $20—couldn't pass up such a bargain.

The aircraft was an old British World War II bomber with four large Rolls Royce engines. It had been converted into a hospital plane and must have been on a return trip to pick up another load of wounded. There were about thirty-five fellow officer-passengers. Once airborne, the engine noise was so loud that there was no talking, but the scenery from the windows was spectacular. While still daylight, we passed a series of glaciers that were slowly inching down mountain valleys into the sea.

It was dark by the time we reached Anchorage. We stepped from the plane into below-freezing weather. My face burned, and I shivered in my light clothes.

Anchorage, Alaska

12 November 1952

I've really been in luck. Our plane was grounded here in Alaska and I'll probably be here several days. This is the most interesting and beautiful country I have ever seen. Huge snow-capped mountains tower on each side of us. Glaciers are in almost every valley. The hugeness of the whole country almost takes your breath away.

This morning I met an old geologist who had just returned from a trip to the Jade Mountain area north of the Arctic Circle. He had several large pieces of jade and I bought one little piece from him for $30. He had made the trip at government expense to get the stones for special services.

There's a Kodiak bear skin hanging in the officers' club. You should see the size of it. The head alone is as big as a bushel basket.

13 November 1952

I'm still in Alaska and chances are we won't leave until tomorrow night. . . . There's a lot I would like to tell you about Alaska . . . ordinary construction workers make from $1,500 to $2,000 per month. . . . Officers get an additional $125 per month to offset the high cost of living.

The days here are very short and getting shorter. It gets daylight about 8:30 and is dark by 3:30. The sun just barely stays above the southern horizon, even at midday. It is not too cold here yet. It gets about 15 during the night and up to 25 in the day. The snow is kept cleared from the roads and sidewalks.

I wish I was stationed here instead of Japan or Korea. You could come up. . . . After a hard day in the stinging cold, a warm little house would be pleasant— ah, and those long nights. Most of the wives here like it very much.

14 November 1952

Anchorage, 6:00 PM: I've only a minute—just received word to be ready to fly in twenty minutes. Our little vacation in Alaska is over. My main regret is knowing that I'm going to be moved farther away from you.

Cold Bay, Alaska

15 November 1952

Well . . . , I'm still here in Alaska, but now in Cold Bay, which is a little airfield at the head of the Aleutian Island chain. It's a long story as to how I got here. . . . From my last letter you know that we were headed for Shemya, leaving about 8:30 last night. About 200 miles offshore over the Bering Sea, one of our engines cut out [actually caught fire]. We put on our Mae West life jackets and spent a tense hour or more thinking about the icy water below us while the pilot steered for Cold Bay.

Soon two support planes arrived and escorted us, one on each wing. One of our plane's crewmen stretched deflated life rafts down the aisle near the door. Even in warm clothes one could last only a few minutes in the freezing waters beneath us. Finally, at about two o'clock in the morning, we made an unscheduled emergency landing at Cold Bay, a small military outpost near the western tip of the Alaskan peninsula.

We arrived without any trouble and stepped off the plane into an icy gale of about 50-mile-per-hour winds, whipping rain, and snow. Whoever named this place sure didn't have to use any imagination. This little outpost has about three hundred bleary-eyed air force men stationed here—all trying to figure a way to get out. It's the most bleak, barren, windswept place I've ever seen. We've got good quarters here, though. The food is edible though not too good (the cook wants to get out too).

After two days in Cold Bay, I decided that being stationed in this desolate place could be worse than going to Korea.

It looks like the war may be over before I get there if this trip takes much longer.

16 November 1952

We should leave Cold Bay in about two hours (its 5:00 PM here, 10:00 PM in Dallas). . . . Shemya is about four hours flying time from here.

I've been in a sportsman's paradise here in Cold Bay. Yesterday I went trout fishing in a 50-mile-per-hour snowstorm. We caught trout until our fingers got so cold that we had to quit.

The banks were covered with fish backbones from an earlier salmon run. Even though small trout were plentiful, I began to worry about bears.

Bears are so plentiful that they have to be beaten off the runways with clubs so that planes can take off and land. Just a few miles from here the largest bear ever killed in the world was taken.

This is the craziest weather in the world. It snows most of the time, but strong winds come along, pick up the snow, and blow it out into the bay, leaving little on the ground. Unless we get stuck somewhere else, my next letter will be from Tokyo.

Shemya, Alaska

17 November 1952

From Cold Bay we flew for four hours to Shemya, a major stopover for flights bound for the Far East. Arriving before midnight, we were assigned sleeping quarters for the layover. The snow was so deep that all living quarters were under the snow.

I just awoke from a good night's sleep in very nice barracks on the tip of the Aleutian Islands. The snow is banked very deep outside and all the buildings are connected by steam-heated passageways, making it very comfortable and warm.

Some of us southern guys took a walk around the outside early this morning. After some of us stepped off into drifts sinking up to our waist, we gave it up. We'll probably be here until late this afternoon before taking off for the last leg of our flight to Tokyo.

Tokyo, Japan

19 November 1952

Eight hours after leaving Shemya, we landed at Masawa, in northern Japan, for refueling. From there we flew to Haneda, the airport for Tokyo. Having left Seattle on 11 November, we arrived in Tokyo on the 19th, eight days later. From the air, Tokyo appeared as a clutter of dim yellow lights, not the bright white lights common in America. Bombing during World War II had destroyed most of the power plants. Probably there was still a shortage of electricity. Having arrived several days behind schedule, new orders had to be cut. I checked into the BOQ at Camp Drake Replacement Depot on the outskirts of Tokyo. I had a week or more to explore Tokyo before new orders were issued.

Well I'm here in Japan after a fourteen-hour hop from Shemya. . . . Dan has already arrived and was sent to a two-week CBR [chemical, biological, and radiological] school at Gifu, Japan. . . . You won't get a letter for the 18th because we crossed the international date line. To determine the time here, just add fifteen hours to Dallas time.

In spite of the money I started out with [$40], I'm getting low. Alaska was extremely expensive, and we had to pay our meals and billets all the way. Of course I haven't drawn my per diem yet. . . . I've got to start processing shortly, and get some clothes cleaned.

Later that evening: *I've had a chance to look around since the note I wrote you this morning. . . . I'm really being spoiled by these Japanese boysans [house-boys]. I took a shower while one laid out a mat to stand on. Then he motioned for me to give him my underclothes. Later they appeared on my fresh made-up bunk, clean and neatly folded. I began to catch on so I motioned toward my dirty boots by the bed. He snatched them up and brought them back shining like mirrors. Boy, this is the life.*

I went to the Camp Drake Officers' Club, which is even better than the one at Fort Bliss, and ordered one of the biggest steaks in the house with all the trimmings. It was delicious at $1.25. The PX (post exchange) here has all sorts of values. In chinaware, the most famous names are offered for anywhere from $30 to $50 per sixty-three-piece set. . . . A jade necklace is about $40, rings $50 to $80. . . . Also, they have the most elaborate purses here I have ever seen. Gold and silver braid on a black background is $25.

20 November 1952

In Tokyo there was activity everywhere. The city was rebuilding after being largely destroyed during World War II. The Emperor's Palace, with moat and walled-in gardens, however, had been untouched by the war and offered a glimpse of the far past. In contrast, taxis roamed the streets in massive numbers at reckless speeds and honking loudly. In the suburbs families lived in neat, closely spaced, flimsy houses. The weather was cool with misty rain most of the time.

On arriving in the Far East Command area, we were required to turn in all American currency in exchange for military script. This Monopoly-type money could be changed for local currency in Japan and Korea, since American greenbacks could not be used for any purchases. All monthly cash payments were in script. Most Japanese merchants, taxi drivers, etc.

accepted script, as did the houseboys. There was an exchange system (maybe underground) that converted the script to yen.

I just finished attending a series of lectures on Korea. I still haven't received any word on where I will be sent. . . . Last night I met a couple of Aggies from Korea on rest and relaxation leave (R&R), just back from the front. They were jolly and didn't think it was so bad. Before I left them, we had six boys, all from some part of Texas telling war stories. One main topic here is how to get out early.

21 November 1952

Well my sweet, your big-wheel husband is living a life of ease. Today I got a hair-cut [by a Japanese] that took over an hour. First, he cut my hair, then shampooed it, rubbed it with tonic, then gave me a twenty-minute massage that was one of the most expert that I have ever witnessed, trimmed nasal hairs, and would have given me a mud pack if I hadn't stopped him. . . . The price of this entire operation was 55 cents.

Theaters held a particular attraction. Some plays were old-fashioned Japanese style, with men playing both male and female parts. Another theater had American-style lines of Japanese chorus girls dancing.

Last night I took in a musical show that would equal any on Broadway. There was a cast of about fifty Japanese, and the show was excellent. Stage and lighting were better than any I have seen even in the US. It included ballet, soloist, dance teams, high-kickers, and best of all, burlesque in the best of form—cost 300 yen (80 cents US).

Today I've been looking at gifts. . . . The quality of the merchandise is excellent, everything is clean, and everybody is extremely friendly and polite. . . . This is like something out of Arabian Nights.

22 November 1952

Today I am waiting around for orders as usual. . . . Yesterday, I went into Tokyo and priced some jewelry. The best bargains seem to be in semiprecious stones—one of the most striking is topaz. A necklace set of beautiful clear golden yellow stones cost about $15. . . . Jade is too high. . . . A string of unmatched pearls is about $30, matched ones from $75 to $95.

My budget was such that I had to skip the jewelry, but bought kimonos for Robbie, our mothers, and my sisters, which were mailed home.

23 November 1952

This morning I talked with Dan by phone [in Gifu]. One of our Aggie class-mates, Dutch Maxwell, was with him. He [Dan] has orders for Inchon as soon as he finishes CBR school. I guess I'll follow him, although I haven't received any orders yet.

Tokyo is a city of seven million people, and you travel for a hundred miles and never get out of a residential area.

The food in the restaurants was safe only if well cooked. Girls were in all the bars wanting GI's to buy them drinks. There were plenty of soldiers on R&R from Korea who were willing to oblige. The Fort Drake Officers' Club offered a less hectic evening.

The Japanese rated everything from one to ten, with number one as the best and number ten as the worst. The number one son was the oldest and most favored child. This was backward compared to some American ratings, for example where the number ten signifies the best-looking girl.

Almost every plot of bare ground around the city was being farmed for vegetables. We soon became aware of the "honey wagons." These were wagons pulled by oxen, carrying huge buckets of human excrement to the fields to be ladled out to fertilize the plants. Needless to say they were very odorous, as was the entire countryside after distribution of a honey-wagon load.

Camp Drake had been a Japanese military post before Japan's surrender to the United States at the end of World War II. The latrines had outhouse-type accommodations, with a long row of circular holes cut at regular intervals along a long boxed-in bench. These toilet openings could accommodate Americans seated or Asians squatting. Under each opening was a barrel-size wooden bucket. I asked a Japanese orderly in the latrine if the honey buckets were emptied onto the fields. He replied, "GI shit number ten—too much paper."

24 November 1952

It's been a slow drizzling rain here at Camp Drake today. . . . I got a pipe at the PX—don't know how long I'll use it, but it helps pass the time away. . . . Chow in the mess hall is 50 cents, and I have a weakness for their hamburger steaks. All the eating places here serve food on real china, being cheaper than crockery.

Today I received word that I would leave for CBR school on 26 November and begin school on 1 December. The school will last until 14 December, and I'll be shipped on to Inchon after that.

More delay!

26 November 1952

We're just leaving for the train to take us to the CBR school. It's about a twelve-hour trip by these slow railroads [with their many stops].

Gifu by rail was about 200 miles west of Tokyo. Aboard the train I was able to get a panoramic view of the countryside. Almost every foot of arable land—both flat lands and neatly terraced hillsides—was being farmed. Occasional stands of trees appeared to have been carefully planted in areas not suitable for growing crops. The train also sped along the shoreline, at times atop rocky cliffs with huge waves breaking far below at their base. Occasionally, tunnels blacked out the landscape. The countryside was serene and beautiful. It was hard to imagine that men from these peaceful landscapes had made up the brutal Japanese armies of World War II.

Gifu, Japan

27 November 1952

Today is Thanksgiving, and I have really enjoyed one of the army's much publicized "turkey dinners. . . ." It's late in the evening here at Gifu (Ge' foo). Today Dan and Dutch Maxwell showed me around the post where I am to spend the next two weeks. It's pretty here, an old zero plane base. . . . [Gifu was the Japanese airbase from which kamikaze pilots departed on their suicidal missions to attack American warships]. The Japanese people here seem very friendly—they are polite and clean, and the little kids very cute. . . . I hope I can draw the per diem soon so I can buy some Christmas presents before leaving Japan. I have to pay for my meals and room as long as I'm here in Japan—I won't have much left by the end of the month.

28 November 1952

Today has been misty, warm, and rainy. Dan is leaving by boat for Inchon tomorrow. Tonight he bought me a steak dinner at the Kibo Club, a special place where the suicide pilots were wined and dined before taking off on their fatal missions.

The club was very picturesque, with carved paneling, sculptures, and elegant decorations. In addition to the club building, there were several acres of carefully manicured gardens.

Tomorrow I plan to spend a good part of the day in the gym . . . , it's in an old zero hanger. Maybe I can get back in shape after all this loafing. . . . Your picture frame "got busted" in my travels, but the print is OK. It seems almost unbelievable that I'm married to such a beautiful girl.

30 November 1952

Dan left on 29 November, bound for Sasebo, Japan, 500 miles to the southwest, where he boarded a troopship for Pusan.

Today is Sunday morning and I should be in chapel services, but some so-and-so stole my cap at the officers' club last night. I can't go anywhere until the PX opens [to replace the missing cap; otherwise I would be out of uniform].

1 December 1952

Today we had our first day of class, studying atomic warfare, germ warfare, and poison gases. After class, I worked out in the gym and feel good because of it now. Tonight the sky is clear and things are illuminated in silvery black and gray by a full moon overhead. Little pieces of clouds drift past the moon. . . . Camp Gifu is in a little valley surrounded by sharp little hills that are visible. Until I return home, I will store up wonders of the Orient to tell you about while we're sitting before an open fireplace.

2 December 1952

During the day the instructors manage to claim my attention, but I must find something to do at night. Tonight I went to the early movie to see O. Henry's Full House, *which was a group of his short stories. The last one was a story of two young lovers at Christmastime. This tender scene brought on just a little wave of homesickness. At least another day has passed.*

3 December 1952

Today I got paid. Also, I worked out in the gym. My workouts have already produced an amazing effect on my misshapen body. I've made unbelievable progress toward getting back in shape.

I had my first exam today and scored a 96. Not bad for an Aggie. It was one of the highest grades in the class. Fortunately they don't count off for misspelling.

In your last letter you mentioned that your old friend, Cliff Douglas, said husbands were untrue over here. He was right. You'd be surprised at the number of apparently respectable men who have started living with Japanese girls. However, you can be sure that I'll never be one of them, even if I'm the only soldier in Japan that doesn't. Furthermore, I think Cliff is a dirty son of a bitch for talking to you like that. I'd prefer that you didn't associate with him anymore since I'm not there to beat the hell out of that cowardly draft dodger.

As to clothes, at Camp Drake they issued me a complete set of field clothes, including another overcoat. In Inchon, I'll get an issue of cold-weather clothing that will be suitable for the arctic temperatures in Korea.

I have been thinking about the oil business when I get home. I think it would be wise to work for an oil company for two or three years then go back for a master's degree. After that, Dan and I could start our own oil company.

4 December 1952

On the exam today, I made a 96 and was number five in my class of a hundred. We went through the gas chambers today—as you can tell, my gas mask worked.

I still haven't mailed any Christmas gifts home other than a few souvenirs. My room and meals take about $75 per month as long as I'm in Japan. I can never seem to get ahead enough to buy anything. In fact, I was short on eating money for about three days. As soon as I get to Korea, I won't have to pay income tax, but will probably be charged $42 per month for food. Lodging in the foxholes is free (so far).

5 December 1952

You have a very tired husband tonight. This evening I went down to the gym and got into a basketball game. We have two full-length indoor courts. After the first five minutes I felt that my lungs would burst. I've never seen such a fast-moving game. Somehow I managed to hold my position for three full hours without a single break. Ah, to be young again. . . .

After a quick sandwich at the club and a hot shower, I staggered to bed and don't intend to move again until morning. I have a nice room here in the BOQ. There are eight officers in here and we have all gotten into the same rut, staying in at night reading and writing letters.

7 December 1952

I'm lying here in bed trying to recover from the soreness I acquired in the basketball game the other night. I've barely been able to get to class and back. . . . Think I will be glad to get to Korea, just to have the satisfaction of doing something worthwhile. Somehow I can't be satisfied with this easy, lazy living, even though I know that I am better off.

8 December 1952

I've been assigned to the 110th Replacement Company in Inchon. Once assigned we were told it is impossible to change. I'm ready to take my chances with the rest of the guys. Keep writing letters. There is no censorship anymore. Enclosed is a picture of me in my bunk snapped by one of the guys."

Much to my regret, I could never get enough money ahead to buy a camera. A 35 mm color camera cost about $25. Later I found that they were so popular in Korea that none were available there, and they could be obtained only in Japan. Fortunately, my brother Dan had one in Korea and provided most of the pictures reproduced in this book.

9 December 1952

I got a letter from Dan yesterday from Sasebo, the port of embarkation for Korea. He has been held over for a week. Today I bought a couple of necklaces for you and a box of cigars for dad, which I will mail tomorrow. . . . Don't consider them your Christmas gift. . . . This Christmas may not be as happy as the last one, but we'll have many more in the years to come.

11 December 1952

I don't need money any more. I've been paid my per diem amounting to $76. If I can find time, I intend to get gifts for everyone. . . . Tonight I went to see My Man and I, *and as usual I got a little homesick. Afterward one of the officers in my room told of his experiences in the last war. . . . They were kind of grim. . . . It gives me a sobering feeling to be going into combat where my decisions may mean the life of some of my men. . . . But then, I'll probably end up running the PX in Pusan and never get close enough to the front to get double food rations.*

13 December 1952

My last day in Gifu has arrived. We leave tonight for a twenty-four-hour train ride to Sasebo. This morning there were graduation exercises for the four hundred students in my CBR school. I sure wish you could have been there. After a short speech, the colonel read off the name of the top honor graduate of the class, with an average of 97.1—none other than your old husband, 2nd Lt. Dudley J. Hughes. I was more surprised than anyone, but I managed to get up and walk out in front of the group, salute, and receive my commendation.

Actually, two awards were given, one to an enlisted man and one to an officer. A corporal's name was called as the top enlisted man. He wore glasses and had a rather shabby uniform.

He stumbled forward to the colonel, saluted, received his certificate, turned, and marched back into the ranks. He had neglected to step back for a second salute before turning. I surmised that he was probably an "egghead," smarter than his superior noncoms and officers, but a "nerd" in the military. This was his moment of glory, his revenge.

I was stunned when my name was called: "Lt. Dudley Hughes, please come forward." After saluting and receiving my certificate, I hesitated. At that point I should have stepped back and rendered a second salute, but in doing so I felt I would be "putting down" the corporal in his moment of glory. I would be acting like a sophomore at A&M. Instead I followed his example and turned without a second salute. West Pointers probably frowned, but I didn't want to be a smart-ass like some of them. After all, there was a war on.

During my stay at CBR school, newly elected President Eisenhower kept his pledge to the American people by visiting Korea. The mission was top secret with no publicity prior to his return. On 5 December 1952, one hour after his plane took off from the Seoul airport to return to the United States, eleven Communist fighter planes attacked the airport.

Sasebo, Japan

14 December 1952

It was an overnight train ride of twenty-two hours to Sasebo. We had sleeping berths to make the trip easier, but food was cold cans of C rations. All the troops on the train were bound for Korea. There was a lot of discussion going on about what to expect. The train arrived in Sasebo on 14 December 1952. The BOQ and officers' club were obviously used mainly by transit personnel, including those going over, those rotating home, or some arriving for duty in Japan.

After a long but not too uncomfortable train ride, I have arrived in Sasebo. This is a typical Japanese fishing village about twenty centuries behind the rest of the world, as is 90 percent of the Orient. One exception is that it has a major shipbuilding industry.

Things are fairly comfortable here, and tomorrow we'll be outfitted for the cold weather in Korea. Rumor has it that we'll leave here Tuesday for Pusan, and go up the Korean peninsula by train. That's the way Dan traveled.

Camp Drake barracks, Tokyo.

Chemical, Biological, and Radiological (CBR) School, HQ Camp Gifu, Honshu.

CBR School, Gifu.

Dan and Dudley Hughes, Gifu.

JAPAN, DECEMBER 1952

15 December 1952

It is a misty, rainy, warm day here in Sasebo. After arriving late last night we bedded down, but got up early this morning to draw our heavy clothing and rifles. We have long-handles, a wool sweater, field pants, fatigue shirts, wool OD [olive drab] trousers and shirts, fur-lined inner jacket, fur-lined cap, field jacket, and overcoat. . . . Tomorrow afternoon we will board a ship for Pusan.

I was issued a carbine rifle by the 110th Replacement Battalion in Sasebo, but it was preserved in Cosmoline, a thick grease that made the gun inoperable until it could be cleaned. There was no cleaning material available.

16 December 1952

Last night I went into Sasebo to the Central Officers' Club. There we enjoyed a very elite six-course dinner. We had salad, soup, fish, a main course of steak, and dessert, along with a bottle of wine. The club is an old Japanese officers' club, very refined, with a very good Japanese band to add atmosphere to the meal. Everything was perfect except for you not being there.

The loudspeaker in our BOQ announced that we must "fall-out" to board the ship this afternoon.

17 December 1952

Last night we boarded ship and spent the night in crowded triple-deck bunks. Word has been passed around that we won't leave the harbor until about four o'clock this afternoon. We staggered up the gangplank carrying all our gear, which now consists of two full duffel bags, despite the fact that I stored almost all the stuff that I brought from home.

I went up on deck later. The lights from the shore were making long sparkling streaks across the black water of the bay. I thought of you.

This morning I watched a troop transport slip out through the early fog, headed for home with a load of Korean returnees. Later another very large troop ship arrived from the States with a very large load of glum-looking replacements.

The trip to Pusan will take about twelve hours, so we'll unload Thursday morning the eighteenth, and we'll probably be in Pusan for a day or two.

At sea Wednesday night, 17 December: *We are at sea in the blue Pacific, and at present we're cutting our way between the numerous Japanese islands that seem to rise on every side [the Strait of Korea]. . . . Up on deck the cold wind is whipping a thin salt spray with some force. It was a beautiful sunset. High streaky clouds filled the sky with wisps of gold with a background of deep blue-gray winter sky. We're scheduled to unload in Pusan at 8:15 tomorrow morning.*

Pusan, South Korea

18 December 1952

Going on deck the next morning, we found the ship edging toward a row of creosote pilings along the pier in Pusan Harbor. Just before it bumped to a halt against the pilings, a small Korean ran out and pushed with his hands against the side of the huge vessel. The ship came to an abrupt stop. Everyone cheered. He jerked off his quilted earflap cap and bowed.

From the ship we were driven to a fenced-in compound with barracks. After getting settled, we were lectured about Korea and the train ride to Yongdungpo the next day. We were issued ammunition for our weapons, as the train had been ambushed on occasion. Frantically, we used toothbrushes and coat hangers to try to clean the rifles to an operational state. Nearby was an extensive UN cemetery with rows of evenly spaced crosses as far as one could see.

Well, we landed today in Pusan. . . . Korea is many times more backward than Japan. . . . Dan left on 8 December for Inchon, so I will have to wait until I arrive there before finding where he is assigned.

19 December 1952

I'm rapidly becoming accustomed to Korea. The most notable hardship is lack of plumbing. It's necessary to carry a canteen of water around with you for drinking and washing. To shave this morning, I had to heat a canteen cup of water on a kerosene heater, then walk a block to a stand with some steel helmets set in it to be used as washbasins. There are some hot showers, but they run polluted water and can't be used except from the neck down . . . so I've cut out showers. . . .

We'll leave early this afternoon by train (if you can call it that) for Yong-dungpo. . . . The trip is a little over 200 miles, but we were told it would take twenty-four hours. Seats on the train consist of wooden benches, and the railcars are little dinky wooden things.

That afternoon, we began the long train ride from Pusan to Yongdungpo. Several of the windows were broken out, and some of the doors between cars would not close. The toilet was a hole in the floor, open to the rails and crossties "speeding" slowly by below. Outside air circulated freely through

Aboard ship, Sasebo to Pusan.

Pusan Replacement Center.

Korean countryside from train.

United Nations cemetery, Pusan.

SOUTH KOREA, DECEMBER 1952

*Kids like gum and candy. Train ride from
Pusan to Yongdungpo.*

Civilians hoping for a handout.

Farmhouse on rice paddy.

Terraced farmland, Pusan area.

SOUTH KOREA, DECEMBER 1952

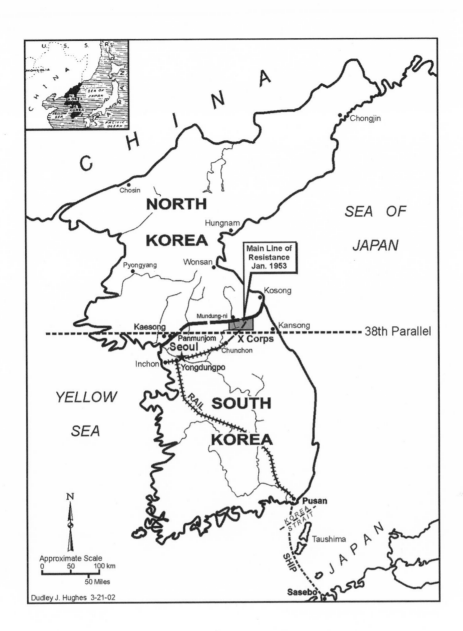

MAP I KOREAN PENINSULA

41

the car. There were about thirty officers in the car, our duffel bags stacked in a large cubical at one end.

The train rattled along at a leisurely pace, passing through Korean villages and countryside farms. In some villages, women with long black hair, wearing long white dresses stood by the tracks with their babies and small children, hoping for food or other gifts from the passing American soldiers. The farmland was terraced but barren and frozen during the cold season.

Dressed in the newly issued wool uniforms and topcoats, we did not suffer from the outside air until the sun went down. As darkness approached, the air turned frosty, chilling exposed flesh and creeping through the inadequate uniforms. Soon the entire group was shivering uncontrollably. It was impossible to stop the flow of cold air through the railcar. The cold became almost unbearable. We piled the duffel bags along the aisle and tried to use them for cover to no avail. Groups lay together hugging each other, trying to help hold some of the escaping warmth. Eventually most became numb and resigned to the prospect of freezing to death. Still, no one could sleep for fear they would not wake. Never have I suffered so greatly from such cold before or after that night. The temperature must have been well below zero degrees F, but the wind blowing through the moving car carried away body heat faster than it could be regenerated. After what seemed an eternity of misery, the rising sun did little to warm our chilled bodies.

Lt. Dick Robinson, en route to the 40th Division, had taken the train ride from Pusan in February 1952. He best described it as "the train from hell" (Pruitt 2002, 422).

Yongdungpo, South Korea

20 December 1952
After a very miserable night trying to sleep on those benches in a train that was below freezing inside, I have arrived here at the 110th Replacement Depot at Yongdungpo (near Inchon).

Soon after sunrise, the train reached its destination, Yongdungpo, the replacement depot for the Korean frontline units. Yongdungpo appeared to be a Korean rail center, located immediately across the Han River from Seoul. We stumbled from our frigid moving coffin and were assigned to quarters, which proved to be a row of squad tents.

My tent was warm with a roaring fire going in an oil stove. The tent had been reinforced with a wooden floor and wooden sides. There were canvas cots arranged in a row. I climbed into a stack of blankets on one of the cots with all my clothes on except for my boots. After thawing out, I slept until late afternoon, then went to the mess hall for the first hot meal since leaving Pusan.

We're sleeping here in very warm squad tents with floors, canvas cots, and heaters. After last night, the Waldorf Hotel couldn't be more comfortable. Planes have been going over all day—they must really be plastering the Commies.

We were issued orders assigning us to frontline divisions. My assignment was to the 7th Division, and I was to leave for the front the next morning. By now, Dan was at least ten days ahead of me. The officer in command of the replacement battalion allowed me to thumb through the orders of those in earlier transit. Dan had passed through on 9 December and been assigned to the 45th Division, halfway across Korea from the 7th Division. The commanding officer was sympathetic when I explained that Dan was my twin brother who had "volunteered" to come to Korea rather than Germany so we could serve together. He had me turn in my orders and assured me that I would be reassigned to the 45th Division. I went back to my warm tent and sacked out again. It was 20 December 1952, with Christmas five days away.

Second letter: *Since I wrote you this morning, I managed to get my orders changed so that I can join Dan in the 45th Division.*

21 December 1952

Today I feel very refreshed after a good night's sleep in a warm tent. Boy, was I feeling low yesterday after that train ride from Pusan. It snowed here last night, and the place is covered with a few inches of snow. Temperatures drop below zero at night but rise above freezing in the afternoon. . . .

I found that Dan is in Battery D of the 145th AAA AW Battalion, of the 45th Infantry Division. . . . This letter will arrive home after Christmas, so I want to wish everyone a merry Christmas and a happy New Year. Tell those whom I failed to get presents for that I'll get them the next time I'm in Japan. That includes you.

Second letter: *I spent an uneventful day here in my tent at Yongdungpo. My orders didn't come down today. . . . Four other officers and myself are here in the same tent. We are some of the very few remaining of the 130 we came with on the train.*

In a few minutes an outdoor movie will start which I plan to attend, being the only form of entertainment we have to look forward to. It may sound silly to have an outdoor movie in sub-zero weather, but you'd be surprised at the assembly of South Koreans, GI's, and foreign soldiers that will bundle up in woolens and furs to turn out for it.

22 December 1952

All night long a steady stream of replacements has been arriving. When I got up about 5:30 this morning, about two thousand of these poor GI's were huddled out in the cold like a herd of cattle, waiting to get into the mess hall [a troopship may have landed]. There weren't enough tents to accommodate them. Many of them just came in from that long train ride from Pusan, . . . so you know how they must feel. Most will move right on up to the front by trucks this morning.

Second letter: Another day has passed and still no orders. . . . Here I am just 30 miles from the front and you can't tell there's a war on except for the unusual prosperity a few Koreans are enjoying with American money and black market American goods.

There was an air raid in Inchon, just 18 miles from here Sunday night. It turned out to be one wheezing old gasoline-driven monoplane that had no mission other than to confirm their propaganda that they were staging air raids on South Korea. Not a bomb was dropped, and it may have gone back full of ack-ack holes. . . .

Incidentally, I've been moved out of the tents into a BOQ in a two-story building. My bunk is so situated that I can lie in it at night and watch the outdoor movie while enjoying the warmth of the kerosene stove. Also, I can heat water on the stove to wash and shave right here inside—can you imagine such luxury?

23 December 1952

I ventured out through the shattered remains of Yongdungpo. Almost every building had been destroyed or badly shot up. There were still shell holes in the streets. Mostly military people were moving about, and all carried weapons. There was an officers' club a few blocks away, but we were instructed not to go through the streets alone at night. Across the Han River in Seoul, I found that conditions were similar, with destroyed and bullet-riddled buildings dominating the city. Seoul had changed hands four times during the first nine months of fighting. Since the final battle for the city, in March 1951, Seoul had been in UN hands, and the South Korean government occupied the capitol building with their leader, Syngman Rhee.

The South Koreans have a few small industries here, even though most of the streets show severe war damage. . . . They burn coal so that the air is filled with smoke and cinders. Black soot settles on everything, including our bunks. On awaking each morning, we all have black streaks over our hands and face. Most of the local children neglect to wash the soot off for several days at a time. Things that we take for granted and don't appreciate back home are rare luxuries over here.

24 December 1952

As days passed, being well fed and warm, I began to get a little impatient for my orders. If I had just kept quiet, I could probably have spent the rest of the war there in Yongdungpo. My impatience won out, and I went to see the commanding officer, reminding him that I was waiting on orders to the 45th Division.

I'm afraid that I will miss out on the merry making and Christmas spirit this year. Here in the BOQ, the passing officers seldom stay more than one day, so there's no one here that I really know. Around the room canvas cots have been nailed one above the other to form double bunks. Most of these are heaped with blankets and coats with a head sticking out of one end. A little Korean houseboy is looking at American magazines and writing things down in their chicken-scratch type writing.

Each night I have to sleep under four blankets, with a wool sweater and fur-lined jacket as pajamas. With the heater staying on all night, I can keep warm.

Tonight we had an extra movie, a double feature, and even a little Christmas tree. The Chinks tried an unsuccessful attack on the west end of the line last night, we were told.

Christmas Day 1952

I've just finished a huge turkey dinner. . . . Maybe the quality didn't reach that of home but the quantity did. . . .

I don't know when I will leave this idle place. There's nothing to do but wait. This little town is so filthy and full of thieves that I only leave the post when it is necessary to walk down to the PX. It's going to be a relief to get up to the 45th Division.

Second letter: *Boy, it's cold tonight, well below zero. I have crawled into bed and my feet are like chunks of ice.*

Christmas Day has been quite pleasant. Besides the big dinner, there was a short chapel service, which I enjoyed, and also a double-feature movie again tonight.

Yongdungpo.

Yongdungpo.

Kimpo Air Field, Inchon.

Ox cart north of Seoul.

SOUTH KOREA, DECEMBER 1952

The 45th Division

26 December 1952

I've moved out today (from Yongdungpo), though not far. I received my orders to the 45th and was moved to the 45th Division Replacement Depot (near Seoul) where I was outfitted with another duffel bag of cold-weather gear.

We were issued cold-weather clothes and combat gear, including "Mickey Mouse" boots and a flak jacket. Also, a .45 semiautomatic pistol was added to my weaponry, along with a steel helmet and liner. The clothes began with padded fatigues, pants and top, padded field jacket, fur cap with earflaps, and a parka with fur-lined hood.

The boots, officially termed "thermal boots," were one of the best improvements in cold-weather gear that came out of the Korean War. A large number of the ground soldiers during the first year of fighting had suffered frostbite to their feet, even to the extent of losing toes or being permanently crippled. The footgear then being issued was World War II–type leather boots with heavy wool socks. By 1952 a thermal boot was being issued that consisted of black rubber inside and out, with insulation sealed between the two layers. The insulation made the boots oversized, giving them the appearance of the shoes worn by the Walt Disney cartoon character Mickey Mouse. With these boots, only a single pair of thin cotton socks were worn. Even at 30 degrees below zero, feet sweated in the cotton socks. These boots were a godsend to combat troops living in the trenches and bunkers. Their only disadvantage was that they had rubber treads, which easily slipped on ice, causing many spills.

The cold-weather clothing being issued was also a great improvement over World War II clothes. During the early battles in Korea, extremely cold weather caused as many casualties as enemy fire. Hypothermia killed and maimed troops not equipped for severe arctic temperatures. The concept of multiple thin layers and lightweight quilted-down outer clothing, learned from the Koreans, replaced the heavy wool clothes of World War II. Fur caps with earflaps kept the head warm in subzero weather and fit under steel helmets.

The personal body-armor flak jackets prevented many casualties from shrapnel or small caliber bullets. This revival from the days of knighthood was made possible by development of strong, lightweight bulletproof fabric. The first one issued to me was a vest with thin metal or fiberglass plates in the lining, which covered the chest and back and was held up by canvas shoulder straps. This was quickly replaced in combat by the new 1952 model, which zipped up the front like a vest and protected the shoulders and upper abdomen as well as the chest and back. It was made of twelve-ply ballistic nylon encased in a heat-sealed vinyl film and contained in an outer shell of nylon cloth—all weighing 8½ pounds. There were many rumors that a flak diaper to protect the family jewels was to be issued, but much to everyone's disappointment, that didn't materialize.

Another absolute necessity, a goose-down mountain sleeping bag with two wool blankets, was issued. Indoors or outdoors, this sleeping bag allowed one to sleep in cozy warmth (but usually with clothes on).

Tomorrow morning early we will move out for the east end of the line about 135 miles away. . . . I was issued a new set of patches to wear. The 45th Division is called the "Thunderbird Division" and was originally a National Guard unit from Oklahoma. [The patch is a golden American Indian thunderbird symbol on a red background].

The 45th Division was the Oklahoma National Guard, which had arrived in Korea a year earlier, in late December 1951, after a training period in Hokkaido, Japan. It was the first National Guard division to go into combat in the Korean War. The 45th relieved the 1st Cavalry Division, which moved back to Japan to resume its former place in the Japanese occupation force. At the time of my arrival in December 1952, the 45th was located near the far eastern end of the MLR, its eastern boundary less than ten miles from the Sea of Japan. The terrain consisted of high mountains with heavy snow cover along the valley of the frozen Soyang River. Before the 45th Division arrived in Korea, heavy fighting by other units had secured the area now being defended.

Earlier Battles in the 45th Division Sector

After the UN Command had halted its advance in June 1951, the "Kansas-Wyoming" defense line was established adjacent to the 38th Parallel. The decision was made to strengthen the defensive line and to confine offensive action to such limited advances as were necessary to dominate the more favorable terrain. One of the earlier prominent obstacles to the Kansas-Wyoming line was a deep circular valley some four miles across, rimmed by hills rising 1,000 to 2,000 feet from the valley floor. The North Koreans held the commanding terrain and used these high observation points to harass the UN troops. This valley became known as the "Punchbowl," a fitting name for such a uniform circular feature.

As a geologist, I struggled to determine what could have created such a valley. The most obvious explanation was that it was a crater caused by a meteorite, possibly millions of years ago. One huge explosion probably created the Punchbowl. Ironically, it had been peppered with thousands of smaller explosions as two armies tried to wrestle it from each other. Those who fought and died there may have thought the Punchbowl was formed by a missile from the devil.

During July and August 1951, heavy fighting by UN forces took one high point after another around the rim of the Punchbowl. Finally, the North Koreans withdrew, giving up the Punchbowl to UN forces.

The UN then attacked a ridge three miles to the west, which came to be known as Bloody Ridge. By 5 September it, too, was taken. UN casualties during this action were 2,772, including 326 killed. Enemy losses were 1,389 confirmed dead from an estimated 1,500 casualties (Tucker 2002, 80).

Eight days later, the US 2nd Division attacked a ridge two miles north of Bloody Ridge. They found an enemy, well dug in with tunnels and caves, that resisted artillery pounding. After thirty days of bloody battle, with several supporting units joining the fight, only the south half of the ridge was in the possession of UN forces. This became known as Heartbreak Ridge. On 13 October 1951 the battle for Heartbreak Ridge was ended, with the Communists still holding the northern portion. The UN forces suffered 3,700 casualties. Enemy estimates were over 25,000 casualties (Tucker 2002, 240). Many less publicized battles for other hills and terrain also took place up and down the line.

The US 45th Division arrived from Japan in December 1951 to become part of the X Corps. When I arrived a year later, other units in the X Corps included the ROK 7th Division, the US 40th Division (National Guard Division from California), the US 5th Regimental Combat Team (RCT) (attached to the 40th Division), and the newly trained ROK 12th Division. The X Corps manned the front line from the Hwach'on Reservoir eastward through the heavily forested South Taeback Mountains, for about 25 miles. These were very steep mountains cut with valleys and deep ravines. The Sea of Japan was visible from high points along the eastern boundary.

The X Corps was part of the 8th Army, which was made up of all the United Nations military forces in Korea. Opposing the X Corps were the

North Korean III Corps east of the Punchbowl and the Chinese 60th Army to the west.

Several topographic features of the X Corps area, for example Punchbowl, Bloody Ridge, and Heartbreak Ridge, had become household words in the United States. On the Communist side was Luke's Castle (usually called "Luke the Gook's Castle"), where enemy troops sometimes assembled for attacks against UN forces (see Map 2, p. 65).

The Soyang River ran south through a deep valley about five miles east of the Punchbowl, where my tour of duty with the 45th Division would begin. Now I would help defend these costly miles of hard-won real estate. (On military maps the Soyang River is shown as "Soyang-gang" as "-gang" is a Korean word for "river.")

27 December 1952 (Sat. 6:45 AM)

It's snowing here this morning pretty hard, but I bundled up and feel plenty warm.

Our movement toward the front began with a train ride to Chunchon, about 50 miles from Seoul. The train was similar to the one in which we had ridden from Pusan. Berwin Nelson, with the 223rd Infantry Regiment of the 40th Division, offered this description: "The train had most of the windows out and holes in it from being strafed, and in February [1952], it was colder than heck" (Pruitt 2002, 221).

The trip was in daylight, and I now had the proper arctic clothing, so I actually enjoyed the trip and the scenery. The 45th Division had its Records Company, which kept the division's paperwork, at Chunchon. I reported there.

28 December 1952

On leaving Chunchon, replacements traveled by jeep or truck toward the front lines. The road ran alongside the frozen Soyang River most of the way. I was shocked to see a group of ROK soldiers out on the river bathing through holes chopped in the ice. Some were stripped down to their waist, washing from buckets of the icy water. Others stripped from the waist down were also bathing from buckets, apparently having already washed their upper body. The temperature was probably near zero. This manner of Korean bathing turned out to be a common sight, but Americans never followed suit.

After checking in at the 145th AAA AW Battalion Headquarters, I was assigned to A Battery. The battalion was authorized 735 men divided between four batteries, A, B, C, and D, and battalion headquarters. At that time, the battalion was under strength by about a hundred men. The commanding officer, Lt. Col. Henry A. Cunningham Jr., told me that my brother was assigned to a platoon of eight quad-50 halftracks in D Battery, which was providing air defense for several battalions of field artillery in Smoke Valley.

Smoke Valley

A jeep from A Battery picked me up and proceeded northward. The driver agreed to stop by D Battery so I could visit with my brother. About five miles to the north we reached Smoke Valley, which was filled with batteries of field artillery. The entire valley appeared to be engulfed in fog even though the sun was shining above the clouds. In fact, the haze was man-made by smoke generators on the upwind side of the valley. Each morning at daylight these "smoke pots" were cranked up to provide a smoke screen to hide the 160th, 171st, and 189th field artillery battalions from enemy observers looking down from mountains to the north. Thus the name Smoke Valley was established. Officially, this was part of the Chondo-ri sector. The quad-50s were positioned on hillsides scattered around the valley above the smoke.

The 45th Division had three battalions of 105 mm howitzers and one battalion of 155 mm howitzers. Each battalion had three batteries that had been beefed up to six artillery pieces rather than the standard four. This amounted to a total of seventy-two light and medium howitzers supporting the division front.

I surprised Dan in the officers' mess.

He said, "Well it's about time you got here. Where have you been gold-bricking while I fought this damn war?"

A few days before, a squadron of navy jets from a US aircraft carrier in the Sea of Japan had bombed Smoke Valley, thinking the smoke was from smoke shells fired by the field artillery to mark enemy targets. The attacking planes dropped 500-pound bombs that plunged into the smoke and tore huge holes in the ground. One bomb hit a 155 mm howitzer emplacement, killing three of the crew. One damaged a mess hall. Ground troops scrambled for slit trenches, foxholes, or any other shelter available.

It was difficult to identify the jets as they zoomed by, dark streaks against the sky. Several quad-50s opened fire. A gunner in Dan's platoon hit one of the jets. Trailing smoke, the plane went down in the sea, but the pilot bailed out and was rescued by helicopter. A stern reprimand came down from the Naval Air Commander of the aircraft carrier for firing on a friendly plane. In view of the circumstances, no action was taken against the gunner or the unit commanders. All the pilots involved in the attack were brought up and apologized to those who were bombed. Such events are unavoidable in war, but thereafter, air liaison officers were stationed with our frontline units to direct air strikes.

Dan's platoon commander, Lieutenant Cushman, had left that day with the platoon jeep to attend a meeting in the rear. Dan, newly arrived from the States, was the officer in charge, which would prove to be the wrong place at the wrong time. After the bombing, Dan's battery commander, Capt. Vincent Cahill, was infuriated that Dan had not gone to each gun emplacement to assess damage. The facts that he had no transportation and didn't yet know all the gun locations were not adequate excuses. As a thinly veiled punishment, he was scheduled to be transferred up on the line to the 2nd Platoon of C Battery. Their quad-50s were dug in along the trench lines with the infantry.

After a brief visit with Dan, we drove a short distance to my battery headquarters. As we rode along, the jeep driver, Corporal Mulligan, grumbled that it was time for him to rotate home but he was unfairly being held, awaiting a replacement. The jeep climbed out of the smoke as it traveled westward. The wide roads, which had been carved into the Korean countryside by US Army Engineer units, were first-class, surfaced with crushed rock but snow-covered in spots. Some of the field artillery guns in Smoke Valley fired intermittently. About a mile east of Dan's bunker, the driver turned up a hillside to a separate small group of bunkers. One heavily sandbagged bunker was labeled "A Btry CP" (command post) with a scrawled, handwritten sign. Inside I was introduced to the battery commander, 1st Lt. Harold S. Whitlock, a veteran of World War II, and to his younger executive officer, 1st Lt. Ehard F. Nutting.

Whitlock was a short, amiable man in his early thirties who had received his commission through Officer Candidate School (OCS) in World War II and then decided to become an army "regular" after being recalled during the Korean War. "Regular" meant that he had elected to make a career of the army, whereas a "reservist," like myself, would be released back to

Rear area.

USO show: Debbie Reynolds.

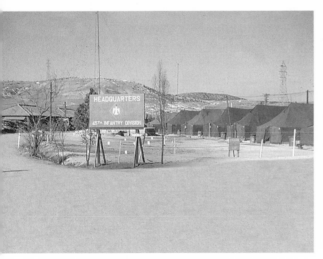

Main headquarters, 45th Infantry Division.

45th Infantry Division School of Standards, Sayong River Valley.

45TH DIVISION HEADQUARTERS, UNITS 8–10 MILES FROM FRONT LINES, DECEMBER 1952

civilian life after serving my two-year tour of duty. I saluted and reported as a replacement, handing over my orders. We shook hands and after a few courtesy remarks, Lieutenant Whitlock proceeded to brief me on the military situation.

A Battery was made up of two platoons, each with eight quad-50 half-tracks. Each halftrack was manned by a crew of five to seven men. These gun crews, plus the platoon headquarters personnel, made up a platoon of sixty to seventy men. With two such platoons and battery headquarters, the battery totaled about one hundred fifty men. These numbers would be higher if the unit was up to full strength. The 40 mm cannons, normally making up one-half of the armament, had been replaced by four additional quad-50s, a more practical weapon in ground support of the infantry.

Even as we talked, the frontline trenches were being taken over by South Korean troops of the new ROK 12th Infantry Division, relieving infantry units of the US 45th Division. The ROK infantry faced two heavily entrenched North Korean Corps along its ten-mile section of the front. Both sides occupied high ground. Where possible, their trench lines were separated from the opposing trenches by deep ravines. The trenches were generally about 1,000 to 2,000 yards apart, forming a no-man's-land between the lines. The ROK 12th Infantry Division was deploying two infantry regiments in the frontline trenches, with a third regiment in reserve to the rear.

Excerpt from letter of 29 December 1952: *President Eisenhower is working toward having all the American infantry pulled off the front lines and replacing them with Republic of Korea (ROK) troops. Therefore we are dealing mostly with ROKs on our front.*

Because the ROK 12th Division had only infantry, the entire US 45th Division remained in place with all the supporting elements. In reality the ROK 12th infantry was "attached" to the US 45th Division, allowing the infantry units of the US 45th to take a much needed rest out of harm's way in Tent City to the rear. The frontline infantry faced the enemy troops, and night patrols often clashed. The infantry suffered more casualties than any other branch of the service and survived harsh living conditions in the trenches and bunkers. During attacks the infantry fought a charging tide of enemy with small arms, grenades, mortar, and recoilless rifles, sometimes in hand-to-hand combat. The ROK infantry was backed by artillery, tanks, and quad-50s, and by medical and other support units of the US 45th Division.

Republic of Korea troops were being trained to take over the task of defending their country as fast as possible in hopes that US troops could eventually withdraw and return home. Replacing the infantry was the first step, while artillery, armor, air, and other support units were still being trained.

The intermeshing of American with ROK troops began in the trenches, where the US 45th Division had artillery forward observers (FOs) in observation bunkers along the trench lines (with interpreters) to direct artillery fire against the enemy targets. In positions immediately behind the trenches were 45th Division medium tanks, usually one company of seventeen tanks in support of each infantry regiment. These were dug in or hidden behind the first ridge behind the trenches. Spaced along with the tanks were some of the quad-50 halftracks, placed in position to deliver direct fire into no-man's-land and enemy trench lines. Scattered along with the tanks and quad-50s were giant searchlights to illuminate the battlefield at night.

One of Whitlock's platoons (the 2nd), armed with eight quad-50 halftracks, was in support of the ROK 37th Infantry Regiment holding the west end of the division's line. He assigned me to this platoon, under the command of 1st Lt. James (Jim) Baker. The platoon's halftracks were disbursed along the five miles of the front being defended by the ROK infantry regiment.

East of the ROK 37th was the ROK 51st Infantry Regiment. A quad-50 platoon from C Battery was in ground support of this regiment. Dan was being transferred to this frontline unit. Of the eight platoons in our battalion, Dan and I would be in the two frontline platoons supporting the ROK infantry, while the other six platoons, including Whitlock's other platoon from A Battery and the other platoon from C Battery, were farther back, in air defense of American support units.

The 45th Division artillery was beefed up with four battalions of field artillery, which filled the valley for several miles to the rear. Closest to the front were three battalions of 105 mm howitzers. Farther down the valley was one battalion of larger 155 mm howitzers. Air cover was furnished by the US Air Force from Japanese and Korean airfields and by navy fighters from aircraft carriers.

Since essentially all the fighting was at night, the final part of Whitlock's briefing concerned experimenting with methods of quad-50 indirect fire. The quad-50s could not be used when gunners could not see the enemy targets. At the time, I only vaguely understood any significant advantage of indirect fire.

When we finished the briefing, darkness had set in. We had a quick dinner at the field artillery's mess hall, and Lieutenant Whitlock gave me a bottle of scotch as a welcome to his unit. Beer or wine was about all I had ever drunk, but I was grateful for this welcoming gesture.

Excerpt from letter of 28 December: *Well, I've finally reached my unit, Battery A of the 145th AAA AW, 45th Infantry Division. Dan is scheduled to be switched up to Battery C, which is adjacent to A, so we'll see each other more often. . . . Tonight I'm here in my battery headquarters, which is a cabin of pine logs half-buried underground and covered with sandbags. Tomorrow I go up to my platoon.*

Tonight the artillery around us is banging away, but it's all headed the other way [outgoing]. . . . The entire division of sixteen thousand men averages less than one killed per day, which is relatively safe.

At full strength, the 45th Division was authorized 17,700 men, 141 tanks, 72 howitzers, and 64 M-16 quad-50s.

The Platoon

29 December 1952

Boy, am I tired this afternoon. Climbing around on these Korean Hills is no picnic, especially with all the clothes and weapons we have to carry. Today it has been snowing most of the day. My battery CO [commanding officer], Lt. Whitlock, and platoon leader, Lt. Baker, and I have gone up and down the lines looking over gun positions. . . . We're operating in some of the highest mountains in Korea.

Early that morning, Lieutenant Whitlock and I had driven about three miles to my platoon headquarters to pick up Lieutenant Baker. I dropped off my duffel bags and met Baker. The BOQ bunker was about 30 feet below the road on the reverse slope of the steep ridge. The roof extended out from a cut in the hill, with the bunker being partly underground. Some 40 feet east of the BOQ bunker was a larger bunker that was the platoon command post, along the same cut in the ridge. This was the nerve center of the platoon, operated by NCOs and enlisted men.

First Lt. Jim Baker was from Queens in New York City. He was easygoing with a perpetual mischievous grin. His accent and mannerisms differed from my Texas background. Even so, we immediately hit it off.

155mm howitzer emplacement.

Ready for inspection.

Dan at 105mm howitzer.

After a night of firing.

ARTILLERY EMPLACEMENTS, 160TH BATTALION FIELD ARTILLERY,
SMOKE VALLEY, WINTER 1952–53

Whitlock's driver first drove westward uphill, along the road carved on the reverse slope of the ridge, for about a mile to gun #1. This was the most westerly position and was our highest firing point on the west end of the line. A deep slot had been blasted through the top of the ridge. The half-track was backed into the slot, its guns pointed out over the valley at the enemy trenches. The Communist trenches stood out as a continuous dark line in the snow on the hillside about 1,500 yards away. My gun #1 was on a high ridge about 500 yards behind our trench line. (Guns were actually labeled in three digit numbers, but single numbers substituted herein are easier to follow.) In this mountainous part of Korea, the valley might lie 500 to 1,000 feet below the trench lines, but here it was only a few hundred feet lower.

A camouflage net covered the front of the slot, hiding the halftrack from enemy observers. About 30 yards farther west, a second slot had been cut through the ridge; this one housed a huge searchlight of the type seen in movies of the blitz of London during World War II. This was part of the Battlefield Illumination Unit. These carbon-arc lights sent a strong beam of light as much as 30,000 feet into the sky to spot enemy bombers for anti-aircraft guns. This particular searchlight was pointed across no-man's-land to a pass on the west side of Luke's Castle, the likeliest route of a North Korean attack.

I asked: "Lieutenant, when you turn on that light at night, doesn't it draw a lot of fire?"

"Yeah, but they never hit us, even when we burn it all night. The beam crosses at a focal point that can be moved inward or outward as much as several hundred yards out front. From the other side, it looks like the spot where the light is located. The gooks [North Koreans] waste a lot of mortar rounds trying to knock it out, all of them exploding way out in front. Sometimes we cut it off to make them think they had a hit. A few minutes later we turn it back on. It drives them crazy. Your gun is safer here than anywhere else along the line."

He called the light Moonbeam. I never knew if that name applied only to this single light—his unit—or all the searchlights up and down the line. During daylight hours it was enclosed in a canvas cover and the entire location was covered with overhead camouflage nets. I learned later that on overcast nights they could shine the searchlight on the clouds to reflect off them like moonlight. This would effectively light up a large area, sometimes for miles.

View from quad-50 in air defense position.

Quad-50 CP in air defense of field artillery.

First Lt. James (Jim) Baker.

Quad-50 position.

SMOKE VALLEY, DECEMBER 1952

Next we drove back east about one mile toward our bunker, or "hootchie," to gun #2, just below the crest of a ridge and only some 150 yards from the platoon CP. The squad bunker was built into the back of the ridge about 20 feet below the ridge line. An ammunition bunker was carved into the hillside approximately 30 yards away.

Contrary to what I expected, the halftrack was not ready for action, but was parked in front of the squad bunker. Baker explained that it was necessary to keep the gun out of sight during daylight hours and to drive it up onto the ridge in firing position at dusk. Unlike gun #1, most of the guns had to be pulled up at sundown and pulled back down before sunrise to avoid detection. Gun #3 was about 100 yards northeast of gun #2, and gun #4 was some 200 yards east of #3. We went on down the line, inspecting the guns and meeting the squad sergeants and crews.

My platoon's eight quad-50 halftracks were divided into two sections (see Map 2, p. 65). Each gun crew operated as a separate squad. The first section of four halftracks, which we had just visited, plus our platoon CP, were positioned along low ridges south of a tributary of the Soyang River Valley. The MLR ran along this stream, west to east, but took a turn almost due north opposite the location of gun #4. It then ran north for about three miles before turning back east along the Soyang River. This bending of the MLR was to put Hill 812 on the UN side. The second group of four halftracks were on a high knoll about two miles north of the first group in a position to defend Hill 812, a prominent high point that the North Koreans would like to possess. On Map 2, these are marked "Sgt. Main."

After leaving gun #4, we had traveled for about two miles, crossing the frozen tributary stream, when the jeep began to grind up a very steep hill. The road was extremely steep all the way to the summit. At the top of the hill, guns #5, #6, #7, and #8 were clustered only a few hundred feet apart. Some were dug in and heavily sandbagged.

Each of the gun squads had a couple of Koreans in their crews. The Koreans were from the Republic of Korea Army and were attached to the squads to learn our techniques. Officially each was called a KATUSA, which meant Korean Augmentation to the US Army. Our battalion had a total of ninety-one KATUSA personnel when I arrived. The 45th Division as a whole was allocated twenty-five hundred. My platoon had about fifteen KATUSAs. The KATUSAs bolstered the fighting strength of our units while receiving training that they could pass on to other ROK troops. They were all attempting to learn English. In addition to the KATUSAs, each squad had

Rear view of 2nd platoon, CP, A Battery.

The author in bitter cold.

BOQ and FDC, 2nd Platoon, A Battery (northwest view).

First Lt. Jim Baker.

SMOKE VALLEY, WINTER 1952–53

Morning gun check.

Inspection by major.

*Daytime cover and camouflage for
Moonbeam, carbon-arc searchlight
for battlefield illumination.*

*Gun #3 squad: the Korean was one of
the many ROK soldiers assigned to
American units.*

SMOKE VALLEY, 2ND PLATOON, A BATTERY, JANUARY 1953

one or more younger (twelve- to seventeen-year-old) Korean civilian house-boys (older boys were inducted into the Korean army).

Sergeant Main, our platoon sergeant and senior NCO, was in charge of the northern four-gun section. The lack of trees indicated that this hilltop had seen a lot of action. Enemy trenches looked much closer. To the west the North Korean trench lines went up and over a high ridge out of sight. The top of the ridge was Hill 812, held by the ROK infantry regiment that we were supporting. We could see a more distant crest on the ridge about 2,000 yards to the west of Hill 812, which was known as Luke's Castle. It was a higher rocky mound, held by the North Koreans, with the silhouette of an ancient castle.

Sergeant Main and I came from the same part of East Texas. He recognized my name from past stateside conversations with his relatives. Two were farmers who lived in the Neches River bottom near Palestine and did contract work for my father during the winter. Both lived frontier-style in the deep woods, in unpainted houses with no running water or electricity, using coal-oil lamps—primitive, even for the 1950s. They had taught my brother and me coon hunting with dogs, and other country sporting activities that are virtually a thing of the past today. Baker confided that Sergeant Main had become regular army after serving in World War II and had served a three-year tour in Japan. It was rumored that he fell for a Japanese girl and didn't want to go home. Instead he had volunteered for a tour in Korea to be eligible for another tour in Japan afterward.

While we were inspecting the guns, we were startled by a faint "swish-swish-swish," followed by a loud "CRUMP," an incoming mortar round. Everyone dove into the nearest slit trench or foxhole, as the nearest bunker was some distance away. My heart was pounding. Several more followed—CRUMP-CRUMP-CRUMP. My first baptism by enemy fire left me shaking, wondering if the next round would land in my trench.

Sergeant Main had left his steel helmet in his bunker. One of the two civilian houseboys with us jumped out of his trench, ran the distance to the bunker, and returned with the helmet, as several more mortar rounds came in. Main said, "Quan, you number one houseboy, but if you ever do that again I'll whip your little ass." The fourteen-year-old boy only grinned. I felt like a coward.

Continuation of letter of 29 December 1952: *Now there are only two of us lieutenants living in the sandbagged cabin* [the platoon BOQ bunker]. *We have a kerosene [diesel] stove and most of the comforts of home, or at least of*

Taking cover behind Hill 799.

Tanks on ridge, firing on enemy trenches.

Dan with tank.

Tank, direct fire, Hill 799.

TANKS SUPPORTING ROK INFANTRY, SMOKE VALLEY, JANUARY 1953

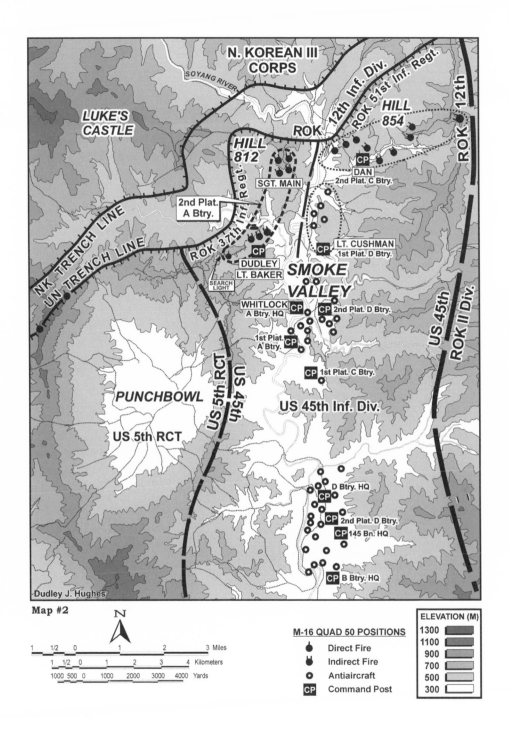

Map #2

N

1	1/2	0	1	2	3 Miles

1	1/2	0	1	2	3	4 Kilometers

1000	500	0	1000	2000	3000	4000 Yards

M-16 QUAD 50 POSITIONS

● Direct Fire
♣ Indirect Fire
⊙ Antiaircraft
CP Command Post

ELEVATION (M)	
1300	
1100	
900	
700	
500	
300	

MAP 2 SMOKE VALLEY, JANUARY 1953

65

a good hunter's cabin. We're going back to battalion headquarters for a while tonight—it's about eight miles to the rear.

After inspecting the guns, Whitlock dropped Baker and me off at our bunker. We took our platoon jeep back to battalion headquarters for the meeting and were given the first of a series of instructions in map reading and indirect fire that evening. As our jeep driver made his way to the rear, it was snowing heavily. My brother, Dan, was there with most of the other platoon officers. A field artillery instructor showed us how to spot our guns and the targets by coordinates on the maps. He pointed out that the field artillery pieces in Smoke Valley are in permanent surveyed locations, whereas the quad-50s are usually pulled off the ridge during daylight and moved back up after dark. The quad-50s' location may be different each night. His idea was that we could fire a burst, then let the forward observer lead us to the target by estimating distance between the observed burst and the target. For example, "up 100 yards, left 50 yards, etc."

At Texas A&M, Dan and I had taken courses in surveying. It seemed to me that if we surveyed and marked the positions and alternate positions used by the quad-50s, we could fire directly at targets by knowing their coordinates alone. I asked the instructor if it would help if we surveyed in our gun positions.

He said, "It certainly would. Also, you'll need the exact altitude [elevation] of the piece to make correction for the target being higher or lower than the gun."

"Could you loan me some surveying instruments?"

"Sure," he replied. "Do you know how to use them?"

"Yeah, I had all that type of training in college. Do you have some benchmarks near our guns?"

"I'll give you a map showing where they are." He seemed pleased at the prospect of having the quad-50s being positioned the same as the field artillery pieces.

When we got back to the bunker, Baker pointed me to the top bunk. I crawled into the sleeping bag without undressing, but wedged the barrel of my loaded .45 between two logs over my head, within easy reach. Regardless of the roar of artillery overhead, sleep came quickly.

30 December 1952

The next morning was calm. Awakening from sleep, I took a few moments to realize where I was. Guns that had been firing the night before were now silent. Looking around, the bunker proved to be one room, about 15 by 30 feet, made of logs, with layers of sandbags and rock on the outside. The north wall was cut into the back side of the ridge, out of sight of the enemy, and offered the best protection for the bunk in which I was lying. A gasoline lantern, still lit, gave off a bright bluish light with a steady hissing sound. In the center of the room was an oil stove, also hissing as it put out heat. A black stovepipe chimney ascended through the roof. On top of the stove a pot of coffee was brewing.

The downhill wall had two plastic-covered horizontal slit windows immediately under the eaves. The floor was hard-packed dirt that had been swept. There was a small table with two chairs, and two jerricans of water sat on the floor nearby. The only exit was a single wooden door made from shell cases, with a small glass panel. This was the officers' bunker. The headquarters personnel were in the platoon CP bunker nearby. In Korea, bunkers were called hootchies. Even in official military reports the word *hootchie* was sometimes used.

Breakfast was a smorgasbord of canned C rations. I chose the ham and eggs, but all flavors had a similar canned taste. Each C ration can had a key that, when twisted, would roll up a narrow strip of metal to open the can. We heated them on the oil stove. One tasty item in the C rations was canned chocolate milk. Heated, the drink actually tasted like hot chocolate.

In order to shave, water was heated in a canteen cup on the stove, then poured into a steel helmet. This was the lap of luxury compared to the conditions of troops fighting in similar bitter cold during the first winter of the war.

Outdoors the bright sun reflected off the snow. The mountainous scenery was breathtaking but steely cold. The larger CP bunker, containing the platoon headquarters group, was about 40 feet east of the officers' bunker but along the same cut in the hillside. It was home for the platoon sergeant, his assistant, our jeep driver, telephone operator, telephone line repairmen, medic, mechanic, and two Korean houseboys—altogether about ten people. The two bunkers were on the reverse slope of a steep ridge about 700 yards behind the UN frontline trenches.

The warm bunkers attracted packs of huge rats, in from the outside cold. They lived in the walls between the logs and the sandbags. No food could be left out, and sometimes in the still of the night they scurried about in our living area. A hootchie that burned was host to hundreds of rats that fled from the fire. These pests carried fleas that sometimes transferred to humans, spreading hemorrhagic fever, which caused bleeding through the skin and eyes. We battled the rats with traps tended by the houseboys, but it was a losing battle. One night I awoke to find a rat sitting on the end of my bunk. I reached for my .45 and aimed it at the rat, then had second thoughts. It would splatter blood or the bullet might ricochet. I could do no more than shoo him away—the rat won that battle too.

Out the door of our hootchie, steps were carved into the hillside, leading up to the gravel road and jeep bunker about 30 feet above. Behind our hootchie, along the cut in the ridge about 30 feet west of the officers' bunker, was the latrine, an outdoor toilet made of shell boxes. On the outside was a urinal, actually a brass artillery shell case, which stuck out of a patch of yellow ice and snow. Inside was a typical outhouse seat with a covered hole. The cover sported a heavy beard of ice crystals on its underside, formed by steam rising from below. Bare skin stuck to the icy seat. The latrine door opened to a panoramic view of the valley below. The trees had suffered from eighteen months of shelling. There were hardly any trees unscathed; they all suffered missing tops, broken limbs, bleeding sap, or other deformities. Still, the hillsides were generally green, unlike the Communist side, where the ground had been churned by repeated shelling until there were no trees left at all, only bare ground.

Excerpt from letter of 31 December 1952: *I have been so busy that I didn't get to write yesterday. We started out early in the morning, surveying in our gun positions. . . . Last night I had to go in to battalion headquarters for another two-hour class on map reading. Afterward, I stayed for a movie,* The Merry Widow *with Lana Turner—very good.*

I didn't realize it at the time, but we were the only platoon in the battalion to begin surveying in our guns in preparation for conducting experimental indirect fire with the quad-50s.

31 December 1952

I'll probably do some more surveying today, and then Baker and I will probably go into the battalion to get paid and take a shower. . . . It's actually very beautiful country with rugged terrain and pine-covered slopes. The snow covers the ground in most places and the streams are frozen solid.

After I had worked most of the day completing the survey to determine the map location and elevation above sea level of each gun position, Whitlock called to ask me to come to the battery CP and stay for dinner. Late in the afternoon, Baker and I had our driver take us to the battalion to pick up our pay. We didn't have time for a shower. Afterward, Baker dropped me by battery headquarters to visit with Whitlock, while he went on to a New Year's celebration at one of the artillery units. Whitlock suggested that I begin calling him "Whit," which was an indication that he approved of what I was doing. He then wanted to discuss a modification to the guns that would be necessary for indirect firing of the weapons. He indicated that the engineers were designing a directional scale to be fastened around the base of each turret that would be available within a day or so. Also, the artillery was furnishing us with gunner's quadrants for setting the elevation.

After one cocktail and dinner at the artillery mess, Whit ordered his jeep driver, Corporal Mulligan, to "take Lt. Hughes to his hootchie, but first, detour by way of Sergeant Main's to drop off these three gunner's quadrants."

Corporal Mulligan violently objected, "No one can get up that road at night!" Whitlock bristled—obviously they had argued before.

"That's an order, now carry it out."

Mulligan fumed but reluctantly took the three leather-cased instruments and placed them on the floorboard of the jeep. We drove off with the dim "blackout lights" of the jeep barely lighting the road enough to see. The speed limit was 10 mph after darkness. By standing orders, the jeep roof was off and the windshield down for quick escape in the event of shelling. A tank rumbled out of the darkness, seeming to barely miss the jeep. The loud rolling "B-R-O-O-O-M-M" of the field artillery pieces in the valley alongside the road reached a crescendo that would last most of the night. Heading north up the valley, we passed more 105 mm howitzers adding to the barrage. About two miles north of the battery headquarters we crossed the bridge over the frozen Sayong River, then continued north up a steep snow-covered mountain road. Even with chains, the jeep slithered back and forth on the slippery road.

The snow reflected faint white light from the brilliant starlit sky and full moon, which made the whole scene marginally visible. The road was carved into the side of a ridge with a deep gorge on the left side. After a half-mile or so up the steep ridge, the jeep suddenly began slipping sideways toward the deep ravine, wheels spinning. At the brink of the drop-off into darkness, the driver stopped and killed the engine. Carefully we got out while the vehicle teetered on the icy edge. If we attempted to move the jeep it would probably slide over the side. Mulligan radioed battery headquarters and asked for a truck with a winch.

We discovered that the bank on the uphill side of the road from us was a frozen waterfall. The temperature was about 20 degrees below zero. Running water had formed a solid sheet of ice across the road for some 50 yards. The Mickey Mouse boots slipped on the ice when we tried to move, so we waited against the ice bank. Out of the darkness from the bottom of the ravine 100 yards up to the right, mortar rounds were being fired at enemy targets. We could hear a dull "CHUCK" when the mortar round left the tube and see sparks trailing from it as it cleared the top of the gulch and disappeared into the night sky. I wondered if the enemy might see the sparks and send in return fire. Apparently they could not, since there was no response during the time we were there. Farther up the road we could hear an occasional abrupt "CRUMP," the sound made by incoming rounds. Overhead, the massed field artillery fire from the valley kept a constant stream of outgoing volleys rumbling toward the enemy. The constant roar had the sound of a train passing above a highway overpass.

We were startled by shadows moving in the darkness. I quietly pulled back the bolt of the carbine to put a round in the chamber. A Korean soldier in a drab quilted uniform appeared out of the darkness plodding down the hill. He was followed, single file, by a long line of similar figures. The Koreans moved with a slow deliberate gait. Their weapons were slung over their shoulders, and apparently they were friendly. They ignored us. There were no features in the dim light to distinguish friend from foe. As each Korean reached the icy patch, they held onto the jeep to keep from slipping. The line of Korean soldiers making their way down the hill seemed endless.

Soon, walking wounded, some bandaged, appeared in the line. Eventually one came along carrying a one-legged comrade, a heavily bandaged left leg missing below the upper thigh. As he reached the icy spot, with both hands busy, one holding the good leg and one holding the stub, he slipped. The one-legged man came loose, landed on his back, and shot down the mountain road like a toboggan until he was out of sight The other Koreans roared with laughter all up and down the line. We never knew if the guy survived or not. It was obvious by now that the ROKs were still positioning their frontline infantry as they took over from the US 45th Infantry Division. We learned later that this was at the end of the ROK takeover, scheduled 27–30 December 1952. The wounded may have stumbled into a minefield during the move.

The heavy artillery fire was screening this final changing of the guard, but also adding to the New Year's Eve celebration. At midnight all the artillery pieces fired at once, creating a deafening roar overhead. That was the nearest thing we got to fireworks.

In the midst of all this, a truck came roaring up the mountain loaded with fresh ROK troops, probably twenty or more men under the canvas canopy in the rear. As it hit the ice patch, it skidded just as the jeep had, but did not recover before it went, tail first, off the road into the ravine. From about 50 feet down, the blackout lights shone straight up. No one attempted to help them, or could have for that matter. Koreans continued to file by, only casting glances at the dim lights shining up from the gully.

Eventually our help arrived. The rescue truck ran a long cable to our jeep bumper and winched us back to less slippery ground as we helped guide it away from the drop-off. We did not try to go up the hill again that night. Instead we drove back down the icy road past the unending file of Koreans, then headed up the western ridge road for about a mile to platoon head-quarters. By then it was past four o'clock in the morning. It was New Year's Day, and the firing was slowing. It had been one hell of a night. Through it all I had been anxious but surprisingly calm. When we unloaded from the jeep, we found only two of the gunner's quadrants. The other had been pilfered by one of the ROKs working their way down the icy hill.

Excerpt from letter of 2 January 1953: *Yesterday I was so busy I didn't get to write, and on New Year's Eve I had to work all night. Remind me to tell you about how we slid a jeep all the way down a mountain side by hand when the roads froze over. . . . It was a funny experience. . . . On a night like last night when the moon is full, all these snow-covered hills are mighty pretty.*

1 January 1953

When I woke up late in the day, Baker said, "Whitlock is pissed off about the loss of the gunners' quadrant and is charging it to your account."

"It was his idea to go up that hill last night. I was just a passenger."

"But Whitlock says you were the officer in charge."

I knew this would come up again. Later that day, Whitlock sent six other gunner's quadrants up and had the battery mechanic put the azimuth scale around the base of each gun turret.

2 January 1953

It's a cold morning here. On waking I found that our kerosene stove had gone out during the night. I had to dress in below-zero cold and go out and find the houseboy to fix it. It's glowing red now, so I can write this letter in comfort. . . .

Baker and I are going to rebuild our hootchie today to make it more comfortable. Also, we're going to run in phone lines so we can direct the action of our platoon from our warm BOQ. . . .

Baker's wife writes all her questions on a separate sheet of paper with space below each for him to answer [with the least effort]. Most nights Baker lies in the sack trying to decide whether to write his wife or not, until he falls asleep.

Robbie, I haven't received any mail since I left Gifu.

3 January 1953

I am supervising some of our enlisted men and Koreans remodeling our hootchie. We built an indoor washstand that holds a steel helmet for the basin . . . with hot water from a big bucket on the stove, and even a drain through empty shell cases to the hillside below.

Also, battery headquarters sent out a series of maps, charts, grids, and all sorts of instruments to set up a Fire Direction Center (FDC) in our hootchie. We made two big drawing tables out of shell boxes and set up about as complete an FDC as the field artillery uses.

What we do is figure the angle of elevation and azimuth to set on guns so that they can fire at targets unseen, even at night. It's something new for AAA AW and I really like it. . . . Here's roughly how it works: The artillery observer watches where our rounds fall and telephones me where he wants fire. Baker and I will figure out new gun settings mathematically and telephone them to the guns.

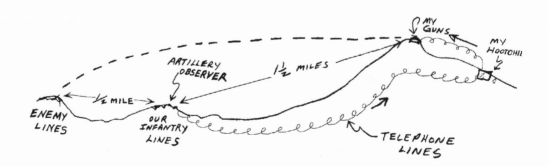

Indirect fire by quad-50s at unseen ground targets, in the same manner as the field artillery, would add a lot of firepower to the infantry regiment. The four 50-caliber machine guns could be fired alternately or together, spewing out murderous streams of armor-piercing incendiary (API) bullets. When used against ground troops the quad-50 was a devastating weapon. API ammunition was designed to shoot down aircraft and packed a wallop far greater than its infantry 50-caliber counterpart of World War II. API had a range of about four miles, 7,000 yards, whereas, the range of the standard 50-caliber ammunition used by the infantry was 2,500 yards. The armor-piercing element could mow down trees plus any soldiers behind them or snipers in their branches. One of the most fearsome aspects of API was the small phosphorus charge that flashed when it struck. Falling among troops, these white-hot explosions covered the ground like exploding hailstones. The quad-50s had been an effective weapon during the mobile phase of the Korean War, as fighting was mainly during daylight hours where the retreating enemy could be spotted. When the armies dug in and fighting shifted to nighttime, the quad-50s became almost useless. For the past one-and-a-half years, the quad-50s had seen little action.

A February 1952 letter by Paul Steffen, an infantryman in the 223rd Regiment of the 40th Division, described early attempts to use quad-50s during night fighting in the trench lines:

> Things would be quiet for a week or so, and these idiots in those quad-50s—you know, those halftracks—would come up to our position, maybe six or eight of them, and they would fire off about 10,000 rounds into the Chinese positions, and then they would take off. We were sitting right there where they had been, and we would catch all the incoming Chinese mortars. (Pruitt 2002, 195)

There were some positive exceptions, as told in the following letter by George Dufresne. In late November 1951, an infantry patrol from the 40th Division was ambushed by Chinese between the lines, in no-man's-land, near the Iron Triangle. After a prolonged firefight, the patrol made their way back toward their lines with the Chinese in hot pursuit. Dufresne was wounded:

> A black guy from Mississippi . . . helped me all the way back across 'No Man's Land' until we got to our outpost.

Just as we got back, somebody with a bullhorn said "Hit the deck!" So we all hit the deck and these lights came on. They had some searchlights and quad-50-calibre machine guns on a half-track. It was the most devastating weapon I have ever seen in my life. I looked back and could see those Chinese that were pursuing us were not very far behind. I could have thrown a rock and hit them. They fired right over our heads with those quad-50s, and just chopped those guys down. The Chinese were going to finish us off with bayonets. They had fixed bayonets. (Pruitt 2002, 58–59)

Developing Indirect Fire Techniques

The following four pages of technical information concern the methods that were developed to conduct indirect fire with the M-16 quad-50 machine guns. The casual reader may find this difficult to follow and of little interest; it has been added largely for its value to army historians and artillerymen of the 1950s.

When a 50-caliber round is fired, the projectile leaves the gun's muzzle at a high rate of speed—2,950 feet per second—but it gradually slows because of friction from the air. Also, gravity begins to pull the bullet down out of its original trajectory, or path. A set of firing tables has been developed that show the angle a gun must be raised to compensate for this drop, the angle being dependent on the distance to the target. A correction must also be made to adjust for the difference in altitude between the target and the gun. This difference—either higher or lower than the gun—is called the "vertical interval" (VI). A correction for the VI is added to or subtracted from the gunner's quadrant elevation. All these variables must be accounted for to fire accurately.

The maximum range of 50-caliber armor piercing incendiary (API) ammunition is about 7,000 yards, or four miles. The armor-piercing ability of a fired round is lost at about 2,500 yards because of the decrease in velocity, but the projectile would penetrate human flesh to a range of 6,500–7,000 yards.

We planned to use the field artillery methods to determine the settings for the guns. Two settings would be necessary to accurately fire the guns: elevation and azimuth. Elevation is the upward or downward angle at which the gun barrel is pointed to hit the target (in a vertical plane). In artillery, elevation is set by use of a gunner's quadrant, which would work on the flat top of a 50-caliber machine gun.

The other setting, azimuth, is the horizontal direction in which the gun is pointed to hit the target, usually referred to as "deflection" in field artillery. For the quad-50s, we preferred the term "azimuth," which is simply the compass direction from the gun to the target. The scales were marked through a complete circle of 360 degrees, in a clockwise direction (the field artillery measures horizontal direction in mils which is 1/6400th of a circle vs. 1/360th of a circle for degrees). For M-16 machine guns, the use of degrees was simpler and sufficiently accurate for our purposes.

The field artillery fire direction center (FDC) has an S-3 (officer in charge of operations) who supervises the operation and makes decisions as to targets. He has a horizontal control operator in charge of furnishing the gun settings for direction, and a vertical control operator who computes the angle (elevation) to set the guns in order to hit the site. The horizontal operator uses a range deflection fan to determine the direction. To calculate the angle for the gunner's quadrant, the vertical control operator uses a special slide rule called a graphic firing table (GFT) that includes correction for any difference in altitude. Other corrections were made, including drift, type of projectile, and powder charge.

Baker was to be the horizontal control operator, and I was the vertical control operator. For firing charts, we each had a map with a one-kilometer grid, topographic contours in meters, and other terrain features, such as rivers and roads. We added our surveyed gun locations, friendly and enemy lines, and other helpful data. Each of our eight gun locations was marked with a blue pin. Targets would be marked with red pins. Having no GFTs, we used the tabular firing tables in the 50-caliber manual. Elevation for the gunner's quadrant was measured in mils, but azimuth was measured in degrees. We had to use a combination of English (Imperial), metric, and military units (i.e., yards, meters, and mils), which complicated the calculations.

Targets from a field artillery forward observer (FO) were given by coordinates on the grid (in yards), which could be plotted on our maps. We used a deflection fan (also scaled in yards) to measure the distance to target (range). The elevation, in mils, was read directly from the tables in the manual for that range. Correction for altitude presented a different problem. The altitudes of our gun positions and targets were in meters, whereas our vertical interval tables were in feet. This discrepancy required converting the vertical interval from meters to feet before we could determine the altitude correction.

The azimuth setting to the target was measured directly from our maps. Relayed to the gun, the turret would be turned until this reading was lined up on the azimuth scale. This would point the gun at the target. Next, the elevation of the gun required to reach the target at that range, adjusted for altitude difference between the gun and the target, would be obtained from tables and relayed. Since the guns were located some distance apart, it was necessary to make a separate calculation for each gun position.

We had planned to copy the field artillery's FDC methods, but soon found that its operation required correcting many more variables than was necessary in 50-caliber fire. The 50-caliber ammunition had a fixed powder charge and single projectile, rather than the several options of charges and projectiles available to the field artillery. It was a high-velocity, flat-trajectory weapon, less affected by wind, and was usually closer to the target than the field artillery pieces. Its purpose was to saturate an area with fire more than to pinpoint a target. Also, a quad-50 platoon had to make do with two men in the FDC rather than eight or ten.

It took us several hours to show each squad how to set the angle on the gunner's quadrant and how to set the azimuth scale. The four 50-caliber machine gun barrels were in parallel. The turret was controlled by two handles mounted steering-wheel style and was very maneuverable. The handles could be turned left or right to swing the turret (and guns) in a horizontal plane. The handles could be turned up and down to swing the guns in a vertical plane. Due to the sensitivity of the controls, the gun crew positioned the gun by flipping the turret switch on and off while setting the gun control handles in a turn. The turret turned in short jumps until it was stopped at the desired azimuth. Similarly, the elevation was set at the required angle by flipping the switch while the gun control handles were held upward or downward. The angle was set when the leveling bubble on the gunner's quadrant was centered.

The gun crews developed workable techniques out of necessity. To begin with, the upper two guns on the turret were fired while the lower two were being reloaded with new canisters of ammunition, and vice versa. They found that with continuous fire, the two upper guns would gradually creep upward, and the two lower guns downward. That was due to slippage of the rubber pulley belts that controlled the vertical movement of the guns. To prevent this slippage, one upper gun was fired in conjunction with the lower gun on the opposite side. This procedure balanced the pressure on the belts, and the guns held their positions. Rate of fire was about eight rounds per second or five hundred rounds per minute (per gun) of continuous fire. Gun pairs were fired in short bursts, followed by a pause, to keep the barrels from overheating and prematurely wearing out.

All machine guns have a common deficiency. The rapid explosions within the barrels heat them to a temperature high enough that the inside of the barrel begins to erode. After relatively few minutes of continuous fire, the interior of the barrel may enlarge to the point that the projectiles begin to leave the muzzle at lower velocities. The result is that the rounds fall short of the intended target and might fall on friendly troops. During World War I, heavy water jackets kept the barrels cool for longer periods, but barrels still wore out. In World War II, the Germans developed a quick-change barrel that could be snapped out and changed in a few seconds—a very successful innovation.

For the US military, the air-cooled 50-caliber Browning heavy-barrel (M-2 HB) machine gun was developed during World War II. Used on the quad-50 turrets, it was designed for quick barrel change. Bursts were usually limited to seventy-five rounds. During routine firing, the barrels were changed after two hundred rounds, which was the ammunition content of one canister. The barrels were then allowed to cool before being used again. During an enemy attack, the spray of bullets could be poured out for a maximum of ten minutes of continuous fire before changing barrels. A special wrench was used to loosen the hot barrel, then only a quick turn with asbestos gloves was required to remove it. A cool one was then quickly screwed in. The whole operation usually took less than one minute.

A barrel gauge was supposed to be furnished to check the barrel wear regularly, but none were available in Korea. A makeshift gauge was made for each halftrack by welding a 50-caliber bullet to a metal rod marked with a scale. Inserted into the gun barrel, it would show the degree of wear. We ordered the barrels discarded at 70 percent of wear.

Guns had to be pulled down from the ridges during daylight. At dusk they were backed up on the ridge to the stake we had surveyed in for each gun. Communications were by a single party-line telephone, with an operator at each gun listening in on the common net (line) and passing instructions on to the squad. All guns were instructed to sight on the highest peak in the enemy's terrain, Hill 1320, a very prominent peak, some ten kilometers northerly, visible to all the guns. To correct gun alignment, we gave each gunner the reading from our map, which should be indicated on the gun's azimuth scale at his location. A piece of white tape was placed on the movable turret, and a fine line was marked above the desired azimuth reading. This process registered all the guns. An azimuth of zero degrees was north, 90 degrees east, 180 degrees south, and 270 degrees west, on each gun. Firing could then proceed.

Early Attempts at Indirect Quad-50 Firing

4 January 1953

Excerpt from letter of 5 January 1953: *Yesterday we worked all day on up until 1:30 this morning, so I didn't get a chance to write. In the past week I've only had time to write three letters.*

Our first attempt at indirect fire was disappointing. Directing the operation from our bunker, by telephone, we ordered the guns to be pulled up on the ridge as darkness approached. After each had set their azimuth markers, the #2 gunner was told to aim his gun at the crest of Hill 1052, a prominent feature, and fire a burst. The artillery FO easily spotted the swarm of incendiary flashes from his observation bunker in the trenches. The miniature explosions stood out like sparklers on the Fourth of July. His attempt to direct the gun to a target from that point was slow and difficult. The data tabulated was of doubtful use for future fire missions.

For the guns to be effective they should be able to fire on any target in range from wherever they were located. The procedures outlined from headquarters just did not work. Their method was based on the assumption that the guns would be moving about and firing from different locations. They had not taken into account that these gun positions had been surveyed and could be pinpointed on the firing charts.

5 January 1953

We have church today [Monday] instead of Sunday because that is the only day the chaplain can come up. . . . Today is unusually warm, which makes our hootchie easier to keep warm. . . . Dan is now only a short distance away so I can see him more often. [Dan transferred to 2nd platoon, C Battery, attached to a ROK infantry regiment adjacent to the east.]

Yesterday I managed to trade for two pounds of pure black beautiful ground coffee. All we've had so far is powdered stuff.

Excerpt from letter of 6 January 1953: *We had to go to a map class back at battalion last night and I saw Dan.*

Since we were firing over friendly troops in the trenches, we had to allow for a safety zone over their heads or risk dropping rounds on them. Manuals called for 20 yards of overhead clearance for overhead firing. We believed that with the greater accuracy of indirect fire, 10 yards of overhead clearance would be sufficient. To ensure their safety, we calculated a no-fire-line on our plotting boards for each gun. If a target was called for inside the no-fire-line, we would decline to fire on it.

6 January 1953

Here are a few pictures I bummed from Baker and Jones to give you a look at some of our little group. . . . We got the communication man to rig up a radio in our hootchie and can have music most of the day [when it was not being used for communication]. I've got to rush and inspect some of our tracks. We're expecting the colonel up sometime this afternoon and things have to be in good shape.

That night we tried indirect fire again, but used coordinates alone to place our guns on the target. We were ready for the real test. The FO picked a target for us "by coordinates," then kept his scope on it while we fired. We pinned the target on our plotting boards. Baker measured the azimuth while I figured the elevation for gun #2. He passed to the squad leader over the phone: "Azimuth 326 degrees, elevation plus 64 mils." Several minutes later the squad leader reported "ready." Baker gave the order to fire. Seconds later the FO cheered: "You hit it right on the nose—give it another burst." We fired again—more cheers.

We made calculations for all the guns on the same target. We advised the observer that we were going to fire each of the eight guns separately. Baker ordered, "Number 1 gun—fire." The FO replied, "Right on." "Number 3 gun—fire." "Perfect." Baker went through all of the other six guns, and only one was slightly off target. The FO said, "This is amazing." Baker said, "Now we are going to fire all the guns at once." He gave the order, "Fire for effect in short bursts." We could hear the firing of nearby 50-caliber machine guns from our bunker: "ACK-ACK-ACK-ACK." The FO was ecstatic. "You have saturated an area over a hundred yards across that an ant couldn't crawl through. You have created a 'wall of fire.'" He began to refer to us as the "ack-ack." The quad-50s were back in business. Word spread quickly.

7 January 1953

We had an unusually successful operation here last night, even though we had to work late, and I am in very good spirits. Our radio woke us up this morning to the tune of soft music, and I was in such good spirits that I felt I must write you. . . .

Food here is pretty good. We have about half hot meals brought up by trucks and half C rations. Everyone has a huge supply of food from Christmas packages—many still arriving. Baker and I start at one end of the line and inspect all eight of our squad hootchies. Each one serves us some Christmas cake or other goodies. . . . Yesterday I got your first letter mailed on 30 December.

By the third night of firing we were "feeling our oats" and decided to pick a few targets for ourselves. The trench lines of the North Koreans stood out clearly on the mountainside across the valley of no-man's-land and were inked in on our plotting boards. The North Koreans stayed in their caves during daylight hours but moved out into the trenches at night. We decided to fire on the trench after dark with the guns targeted about 50 yards apart along the trench. After the guns were in position on the ridges, we gave each their settings. When the last of the eight guns had reported "ready," we notified the FO of our plans and asked him to observe. "Fire for effect!" All eight guns fired at once and poured burst after burst into the night. The FO shouted, "The whole trench line is lit up like a Christmas tree. They're not going to like this." He was right. Suddenly mortar rounds began to rain down along the ridge and around the guns. The guns stopped firing and everyone took cover. No one was hurt, but we realized that we had aroused a sleeping dragon. Luckily for us, the enemy didn't seem to have the guns very well located.

8 January 1953

It's pretty late tonight (actually morning), but I wanted to tell you about some of the funny happenings here today. . . .

First, I'll tell you about Lieutenant Nutting. . . . He is a typical . . . young officer who lets rank go to his head. As battery "Exec," his main job seems to be sitting back in the battery and harassing us by telephone about every minor problem that he can dig up.

This afternoon about four o'clock the battery commander [BC] [having heard of our success in indirect firing] sent up twelve fire missions for tonight. Also, the colonel was to come up and watch our operations, beginning at six o'clock. Since the colonel was coming, the BC sent up a huge bulletin board and several other bits of impressive, though useless, pieces of equipment to be put in our hootchie before the colonel arrived—purely for "eyewash."

Well, the fire missions take about twenty minutes of meticulous calculations on my part and about the same for Lieutenant Baker, for each mission [to bring all eight guns on the target]. That alone would take more time than we had. Also we had but one smokey gasoline lantern for light, so we immediately dispatched the jeep back to the battery for more lamps.

Such feverish activity that went on for the next couple of hours you can't imagine. We had men there putting up the bulletin board and making other changes, while the houseboys tried to clean up the place. All the while Baker would work a few calculations on his board, then I would snatch away the lamp and take it over to mine for a few minutes, then he would take it back.

In the midst of all this, who should call but Nutting. What did he want? To tell us that we would have to stop these useless jeep trips into the battery, and that he had held up the jeep. Baker argued with him for thirty minutes, but he couldn't convince Nutting that there was a war on. . . .

Well, about that time our stove became clogged up with soot from burning diesel fuel. So our Korean houseboys dismantled it while the temperature indoors dropped to zero. . . . With smutty stovepipes all over the cold floor, Baker and I snatching the lantern back and forth trying to get our missions computed to start firing by six o'clock, who should walk in but Colonel Cunningham, Lieutenant Whitlock, and Lieutenant Nutting. Nutting, realizing the havoc he had caused by holding up our jeep, stood quaking in his boots, while the BC (Whitlock) stared icy daggers at him and made excuses to the colonel. Baker and I kept snatching the lantern back and forth but had been able to get only two missions computed and ready to fire.

The BC sent over and borrowed a lantern from another unit, the houseboys got the stove going again, and Baker and I managed to get all our missions on the way, so everything smoothed out. We hit our targets right on the nose, the artillery observers telephoned back, so the colonel finally became quite happy.

After they left, Baker and I laughed ourselves silly at the situation Nutting had worked himself into by pulling his rank once too often. He's Regular Army, so that the chewing the battery commander is going to give him will really shake him up. Ah, life is good. [After this incident Nutting and I eventually became good friends].

Colonel Cunningham realized that greater speed would be necessary to make the quad-50 a really useful weapon. He also recognized that one of the bottlenecks was that map contours and gun altitudes were in meters, while the vertical interval tables in the quad-50 manual were in feet. This required us to convert feet to meters to calculate the altitude correction. The next day the colonel had the entire set of tables converted to meters and a copy sent to us. This was the first in many steps that would reduce the time required to calculate firing data.

9 January 1953

Excerpt from letter of 10 January 1953: *Yesterday I got stuck in the ice up a mountain road and didn't get winched out until midnight so I didn't get to write.*

Early in January, newly captured North Korean prisoners indicated that attacks were scheduled on two prominent hills in our area. One was Hill 812 in my platoon area, and the other, Hill 854 in Dan's platoon area (the hills were named for the meters of elevation at their peaks). On 6 January, Dan had been transferred to the platoon adjacent to mine on the east, the 2nd Platoon of C Battery, with Capt. Charles McDonough, his new battery commander, and Lieutenant Marlow his platoon commander.

Hill 812 had been the target of an earlier attack. On Christmas Day, 1952, three days before I arrived at the platoon, the North Koreans had attempted to take Hill 812. The attack was against K Company of the 179th Infantry Regiment, 45th Division (before our ROKs had relieved them). The North Koreans had begun by raining 250 mortar rounds on K Company's position, then attacked from Luke (the Gook's) Castle with a reinforced company of more than 300 troops. They overran the forward positions, but were stopped by artillery and mortar fire with help from the 179th Tank Company. A counterattack pushed them back. K Company suffered twenty-five American casualties, including five dead, most being inflicted during the counterattack. The quad-50s did little in the fighting, as this was before the nighttime firing methods had been developed and put into practice. Unfortunately, none of this information was furnished to us, and we were blissfully unaware of any pending action.

10 January 1953

It's very late and I'm half asleep, but I know how you like mail, so I'm going to write a few lines. Dan and I got together today and talked over the oil business.

Earlier that evening the colonel in command of the field artillery unit went up on line and called us from the FO's bunker, asking that we fire on targets he had selected. We had already pulled the guns up on the ridge and reset the azimuth scales. He gave us coordinates to a target on an enemy hill. We made the calculations and called the azimuth and elevation settings to the guns in the best position to hit the target. "Ready sir." "Fire for effect." The colonel sounded pleased: "Very good, right on target, but you took twenty-two minutes. You've got to be faster than that." We fired on several more targets and eventually cut the time to fifteen minutes, then twelve. The colonel left convinced of our capability but still wanted the time shortened. Within a few days we could have fire on a target within three minutes.

The Battle for Hill 854—More Ack-Ack

11 January 1953
Today I walked up and down hills to our four guns on the far right in the charge of Sergeant Main. I walk an average of ten miles per day, most of it either straight up or straight down, so that I'm beginning to get in pretty good shape.

Tonight we're firing on a few long-range targets, as usual. Baker and I can get all our computations done, start the guns firing, and get a fairly decent night's sleep, if Nutting doesn't harass us too much. . . .

P.S. How much do you weigh now? It had better be 125 pounds or I'll start sending you C rations to fatten you up.

12 January 1953 (3:00 AM)
You probably wonder why I'm up at this hour of the morning—well, I was rolled out of my warm sack to calculate some more data. Some Communists persisted in getting themselves killed a few miles down the line. If it's not Nutting, it's something else. [This was a gross understatement of what actually happened].

We built a sandbag floor in our hootchie a day or two ago, and it is much cozier and warmer in here [the sandbags insulate the interior from the permafrost below]. In fact, I'm writing this sitting here in my long-handles.

The eleventh of January 1953 had been a routine day. Dan had written a letter home saying "there's not much going on today." Darkness came, and there was not much firing from either side. Baker and I gave our guns a few targets to fire on intermittently, then planned to get some sleep. Near midnight the telephone rang, and Baker answered it. It was the FO. He screamed, "The gooks are pouring through the pass." He began rattling off targets for our guns to cover. Baker was writing down the targets and calling them to me. I spotted the targets on my plotting board and calculated the elevation settings for each gun. Baker could not leave the phone to determine the azimuths, which his job as horizontal control operator called for. Besides keeping in contact with the FO, he had to notify each squad of their gun settings.

"Damn it Baker, you've got to figure the azimuths to these targets."

"How can I? I can't get off the phone."

In desperation, I took over his instruments and began measuring the azimuth settings. I called out the settings for each gun while Baker relayed them to the squad leaders.

All hell started breaking loose outside the bunker. Mortar and artillery fire rained down all around our position and didn't let up for several hours during the attack. We occasionally heard shrapnel hit the outside of the bunker. Soon we had all eight guns firing. The FO had created a wall of fire with the quad-50s, which the attackers had to charge through. He was elated with the results: "More ack-ack, keep it coming."

The attack had begun at our front but was aimed at Hill 854, some four miles to the northeast. Apparently the battle plan was to push eastward down the stream valley into no-man's-land, then break through our trench line at its lowest point, where it crossed the small frozen stream in front of my platoon's easternmost guns (numbers 2, 3, and 4), which were near our command post. This was a good plan because, once behind our lines, our artillery, mortar, and ack-ack could not fire on them since there would be no FOs to call the targets.

Soon the FO reported that the trenches of the ROK 37th Regiment had been overrun by the attackers, about 400 yards in front of our guns #2, #3, and #4. The ROK infantrymen in the trenches blocked themselves into bunkers. Their stovepipe chimneys had wires crossing inside at roof level so that grenades dropped down the stovepipe would be caught, hopefully exploding in the face of the North Koreans dropping them. The invaders could still use satchel charges to entomb the defenders in their bunkers, but did not bother this time, since their objective was Hill 854. The huge searchlights kept the whole scene illuminated but were limited in their ability to shine behind our lines.

With this emergency situation, the FO called for his own artillery units to fire on the UN trenches where the enemy had broken through, something only done as a last resort. Using personnel-type proximity-fuse projectiles with VT fuses (variable timing shells with a radar fuse), air-bursts exploding

20 meters above the ground rain down shrapnel over about a 30-yard area below each round. The shrapnel might cut to shreds anyone caught in the open but would not penetrate the bunkers. A portion of the canopy of UN fire that had been roaring overhead began showering air-bursts down on this section of our own trenches.

This fire drove the attackers from the trenches, but instead of retreating, most of them charged behind the lines and kept moving ahead toward Hill 854. We kept the ack-ack curtain of fire going out front to hinder reinforcements but could not fire blindly on the enemy behind our own lines. To make matters worse, after the attackers broke through, our own artillery was helpless to stop the advance. Only small arms could be used. The attackers successfully pushed northward up the Soyang River Valley. The main attacking force passed about 1,000 yards to the rear of Sergeant Main's guns (numbers 5, 6, 7, and 8). They crossed into the ROK 51st Regimental sector, where Hill 854 was located. This added more confusion to the defenders, as communication between units in separate regiments was limited.

About one and a half miles to the north, the attackers reached the base of the ridge on which Hill 854 was located. From there, an accessible road led up the gentle slope to the hilltop, about one and a half miles to the northeast but 1,000 feet higher in elevation. A frontal attack on Hill 854 against the ROK 51st Regiment would have required charging up a 1,000-foot, steep, rocky incline at the mercy of infantry in the trenches above. The attackers wisely chose the more gentle slope behind the lines to charge the hilltop objective (see Map 5, p. 87).

Hill 854 was in the 2nd Platoon's sector, C Battery, where Dan had arrived five days before the battle. Three of his 2nd Platoon halftracks were actually dug in along the gentle slope of the ridge leading up to Hill 854, in the path of the attacking troops. These halftracks were in bunkers with overhead cover and barrels poking out of an opening in the rear toward the enemy trenches. Suddenly the attackers were swarming behind the three gun pits. The quad-50s could not be turned to fire to the rear, as they were positioned to support the infantry out front. The gun crews opened fire with their carbines. Fortunately the North Koreans pushed on up the hill toward their main objective. The quad-50 squads eventually ran out of carbine ammunition and called the platoon command post for more. One of the officers strapped on as much carbine ammunition as he could carry and ran out toward the gun positions. In the darkness he made it through.

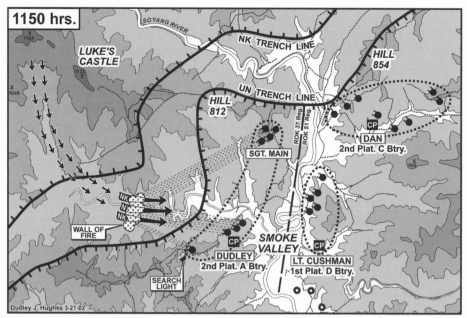

Map #3 Near midnight 11 January 1953, North Korean (NK) infantry launched an approximately 700-man attack from Luke's Castle to take Hill 854. The 2nd Platoon of A Battery, 145th AAA AW Battalion, laid down fire from all eight of its M-16 quad-50 machine guns to establish a "wall of fire" in the path of the advancing force.

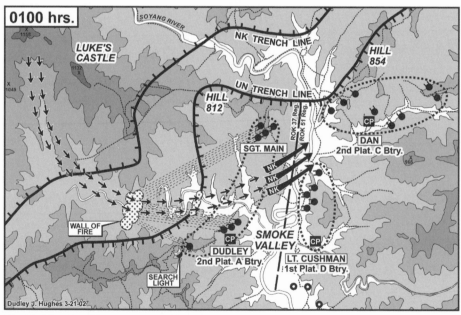

Map #4 Advancing with numerous casualties, the NK forces overran the UN trenches and approached Hill 854 from behind the UN lines.

MAPS 3–6 ROLE OF THE ACK-ACK IN THE BATTLE FOR HILL 854

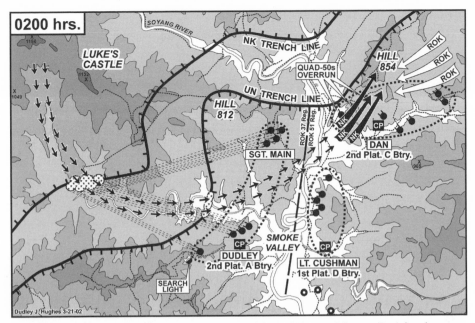

0200 hrs.

Map #5 The attacking infantry overran three quad-50s of the 2nd Platoon, C Battery (Dan), but the squads defended their positions with carbine fire. Advancing to Hill 854, the NK forces were stopped by a counterattack of ROK infantry.

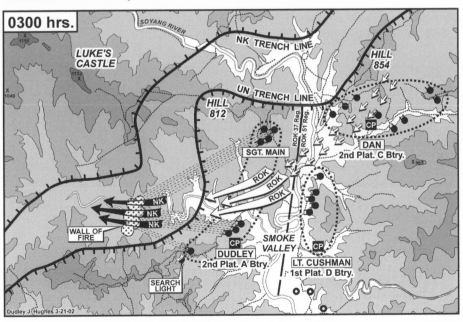

0300 hrs.

Map #6 Forced to retreat, NK troops had to again pass through the wall of fire.

M-16 QUAD-50 POSITIONS	
⬤	Direct Fire
⬗	Indirect Fire
⊙	Antiaircraft
CP	Command Post
⇒	ROK Infantry
➡	N. Korean Infantry

ELEVATION (M)	
1100	
900	
700	
500	
300	

Dan and Marlow were in the 2nd Platoon CP on a lower ridge, some 500 yards to the south of the guns being overrun. With the rest of their CP group, they loaded their carbines and waited for the attackers to arrive. Fortunately, they were out of the main path of advance. The platoon's other quad-50s were farther to the east but equally ineffective with the enemy inside their lines. Some 1,500 rounds of carbine 30-caliber were later reported expended by the three quad-50 squads in the attackers' path.

Of all those in the 145th AAA AW Battalion, only our platoon was set up to do indirect fire. As the battle progressed, the FO kept calling for "more ack-ack." He shifted our targets occasionally to correct gaps in our wall of fire. It sounded like every mortar and artillery piece from both sides was adding to the inferno.

As the North Koreans approached their objective on Hill 854, they were pushed back by a ROK infantry counterattack. They tried once more, then withdrew. Following the same course back, they retreated into no-man's-land. What they didn't count on was the curtain of fire. As they approached their own lines, they had to go through the same wall of fire again. It was terrifying. It was like trying to walk through a rain without getting wet. They were forced to run through the continuous hail of hundreds of incendiary flashes around their feet.

Later accounts from the attackers reported that the quad-50 fire was more terrifying than anything else they experienced during the attack. ROK units estimated over two hundred casualties were suffered by the North Koreans (an astounding 30 percent of the attacking force). These included those hit by small arms fire, the 19,000 rounds of artillery, mortar, and tank fire that had been expended, and the 43,000 rounds of 50-caliber that our platoon had fired. UN casualties were low.

Eventually the firing tapered off and we breathed a sigh of relief. It was hard to believe we had come through with no serious casualties in our platoon. We were given the order to cease fire.

Late the next morning, after everyone had some sleep, I prepared a map showing the route and apparent penetration by the enemy (to the best of our knowledge at that time). Baker and I went to each squad explaining to them the order of the battle and congratulating them on a job well done. By following the path of the targets fired on, it was easy to determine where the invaders had entered and departed our lines. The men were in good spirits and rightly proud of their part in the battle.

About 100 yards in front of gun #3, there was a dug-in tank of the 245th Tank Battalion, also attached in support of the ROK infantry. During the attack the tankers "buttoned-up" inside their tank and waited out the battle, firing as directed. The next morning we discovered a large "potato masher" antitank grenade lying beside the tank. It was football shaped, with a wooden handle on one end and a metal spike on the other. Apparently the grenade had been thrown against the tank but failed to explode. We were taken aback that enemy soldiers had reached within 100 yards, or possibly closer, to our guns and platoon CP. Our hootchie would have been vulnerable to a burp gun attack, having no outside guard.

Change in Tactics

Our first experiment in the use of the quad-50 indirect fire had been on 3 January. We were in a significant battle just eight days later. This battle was the first in which quad-50s were known to have been used in indirect night-time fire, similar to the field artillery (at least in the X Corps). Since, during the battle, all the gun settings in my platoon had been calculated, out of necessity, by a single FDC operator (me), the battalion quickly adopted a change in FDC procedure. One man, with a single plotting board to calculate both azimuth and angle settings for the quad-50s, was quickly made standard operating procedure for all the platoons. This change sped up the procedure and helped us get fire on a target in less time. A second man was necessary to man the telephone (or radio) during an attack.

Probably the most significant development in the indirect fire procedure during this short period was the surveying of gun positions. That allowed the quad-50s to fire on targets without being wholly dependent on the artillery FO. The battalion officers rushed to get the other batteries trained in the indirect fire technique.

We learned much from the battle for Hill 854. Probably the principal thing was the great effectiveness of the quad-50 in ground support, especially using the indirect fire technique. It also became obvious that guns located too close to the front lines were less effective. The great volume of ammunition expended required a change in logistics—many more truckloads of ammunition and tons of brass to be hauled away daily. Even though each 50-caliber hull weighed only a few ounces, the 43,000 rounds fired in the battle for Hill 854 produced over three tons of spent brass. A constant supply of new barrels was needed so that a number of spares would be on hand for each halftrack at all times.

A frontline after-action report by the 145th AAA AW battalion commander, Lt. Col. Everett Light, stated:

Early on the 11th of January the enemy mounted an estimated battalion size attack [700 soldiers] in the right sector directed at Hill 854. Quad .50 support was called for and fire placed on enemy routes of approach and withdrawal. The action lasted for about three hours and the enemy was driven off with a heavy toll of casualties. M-16's of the battalion fired a total of about 43,000 rounds of caliber .50 ammunition in this action. (145th AAA AW Battalion Reports, Feb. 1953)

Information is also furnished in a report on the action written by Walter G. Hermes:

On 27 December the newly organized ROK 12th Division began to take over the 45th Division sector and the relief was completed on 30 December [1952]. The ROK 12th Division received its baptism of fire some two weeks later when a North Korean battalion launched a surprise attack against outpost positions on Hill 854, seven miles northeast of the Punchbowl. Three enemy companies advanced against elements of the 51st Regiment [ROK] and made some progress on the left flank. Pushed back by a counterattack, the North Koreans withdrew. Over 19,000 rounds of UNC [United Nations Command] artillery, mortar and tank fire were hurled into the enemy zone of attack and the ROK units reported over 200 casualties were suffered by the North Koreans. (Hermes, 1966, 377)

A few days of being under fire quickly hardens one to the cruelty of war. Still, it seems incredible that the Communists would sacrifice their soldiers on such a futile attack with no more to gain than a possible psychological advantage at the Panmunjom Peace Talks. The ratio of casualties suffered by Communist troops compared to UN casualties during the Korean War is estimated to be sixty to one. That ratio would no doubt have been true in this battle. Probably this section of the line was attacked because it was held by ROK infantry, but this was a much better-trained ROK force than the North Koreans had overrun in 1950. It was believed that the Communists outnumbered us about three to one. Lacking air support and having their supply lines continually interrupted, they preferred to sacrifice human lives rather than ammunition. The overwhelming bombardments that the out-numbered Americans poured out with artillery, tanks, and other supporting units (including ack-ack) kept our casualties low.

After such a forceful attack, the carrier-based airplanes came in and heav-ily blasted the enemy positions opposite our units. It was quite a show, with dive bombing, strafing, and napalm. We had a ringside seat. To the east of our positions, opposite Dan's platoon, the enemy trenches were shelled by the big guns of the navy ships off the coast. These monstrous shells were much larger than the field artillery's and tore huge craters in the trench lines. My platoon was a little too far west to be in their range.

13 January 1953

Baker has gone into battalion to take a map examination tonight and I'm run-ning the fire direction center. Last night I went in and took the examination. . . . Today I've been taking it easy in the hootchie. It's very cold tonight with fresh snow on the ground.

Dan has gone to Inchon to a three-day school review on antiaircraft gunnery. I will be scheduled to go to it sometime later. . . . Baker and I may get rotated back to the air defense in the artillery valley about the end of the month. I hope not—I like it up here [stretching the truth]. We get $45 per month extra for combat pay and there's no brass around to bother us.

In the valley, we'll just be sitting around doing nothing, wasting time, and putting up with inspecting officers. However, we would be able to get a shower each day and go to the movies every night.

Night before last, about the time I was writing my last letter to you, we were firing missions from an artillery observer [on the front line]. Our platoon was given credit for helping stop an attack, all by long-range firing with instruments . . . with us sitting back in our easy chairs fighting by long-distance telephone and maps.

I'm anxious to know how your job is going [in the constable's office in Dallas]. Boy will we be rich by the time I get back. I'll be eligible to be promoted to first lieutenant at the end of February (sixty days after arrival in Korea), and if I can stay close enough to the front to get combat pay for a few months, we could really stack it up. You should get in five months or more of work. It will take me a month to get home after leaving here. Also, I'll get mustering-out pay of $300. Who knows, we may retire.

14 January 1953

Today . . . Baker and I loafed until about noon, then walked to our four guns on the far right under Sergeant Main. We find a good many things to joke about.

I'm working on a simple plan to code name important landmarks such as road intersections, hills, valleys, and other landmarks after prominent cities. This will simplify and speed up communications.

Our 50-caliber ammunition belts had four API rounds followed by a tracer every fifth round. We decided the tracers were giving away our positions. The squads began pulling the tracers out of the ammunition belts, and we began to fire on targets without the tracers. Soon the mortar erupted around the firing guns, but this time with much more accuracy than usual. We had to stop firing and concluded that the tracers actually made the origin of the fire more difficult to locate, similar to the searchlight beam. Without the tracers, the muzzle blast from the 50-calibers were points of light on the ridge, which could easily be triangulated with pinpoint accuracy. Back to the drawing board—we put the tracers back in the belts.

16 January 1953

Sorry I didn't get to write yesterday, but I was tied up experimenting with a new system of orienting the guns by sighting on the North Star rather than land features. This would enable us to switch positions at night and still orient the gun for firing. Yesterday, we also walked a couple of miles to the Heavy Mortar Platoon which has a PX.

Dan should get back from the school at Inchon today. . . . Temperature at night has been reaching 20 degrees below zero, but I have become accustomed to it. Today we walked to Sergeant Main's position. One of our supply trucks turned over and slid a ways down the mountain road. We watched while they winched it back up.

Tonight after dark we experimented some more with orienting on the North Star. I believe it is going to enable us to move into position after it is completely dark and get oriented for fire. Until now we've had to move up while it was still light enough to see the ground features to orient the gun [the guns are sometimes spotted and draw enemy fire]. . . .

There's something that you can send me that I would appreciate very much. That is about five or ten mantles for a Coleman gasoline lantern. You can stick them in a couple of air mail envelopes and send them in the regular mail.

17 January 1953

This morning I went over to see Dan. He's fresh back from Inchon, so I took him some letters from his girlfriend. He had received a box of fudge from home so he and I consumed it. . . . I walked back and spent the rest of the day doing routine jobs. We've calculated a few fire missions tonight [which are under way].

Outside it's snowing big, soft, lazy flakes that may be the biggest snowfall so far. In the hootchie it's warm and cozy. Baker is lying in his bunk trying to decide whether to write his wife or not. He's been trying to decide for two hours, and as usual, he'll probably go to sleep undecided.

18 January 1953

It's about two o'clock in the morning of the 19th, but it's so peaceful and quiet that I decided to write. So many of our men have rotated home that Baker and I have each had to stand a [two-hour] relief on guard duty [with the enlisted men]. . . .

Earlier tonight I was out at some of the gun positions showing them how to orient on the North Star, when an enemy searchlight came on a few miles away. We'd been trying to get the location of that light for several days. . . . I had the gun sight on it, then read the azimuth scale of the gun. Later, Baker and I plotted the azimuth line on the map. We know it's somewhere along that line. We'll have all the guns watching for it in hopes of getting another line on it. I might add that our side has searchlights all over the place. We can light up the whole front line like daylight whenever we want. You may not believe it, but the enemy hasn't been able to hit a single one of those lights even though some burn all night.

The North Star

Each night we pulled our guns up on the ridges just before darkness to zero them in. Often some were spotted and drew mortar fire. I had the bright idea to wait until after dark and line up the guns on the North Star. In the bitter cold black sky there were usually no clouds. Thousands of stars shown brilliantly, and the North Star, to me, appeared easy to spot. For several days and nights I had visited each squad with a chart showing the location of the North Star, and I was assured by each squad leader that he could identify it. According to the map all the azimuth scales should read the same— 6 degrees east of true north—as the star was millions of miles away and the angle between it and each separate gun too small to make any difference.

This night, after darkness had set in, we pulled the guns up and lined up on the North Star. The guns reported ready. We began firing on targets. The switchboard in the noncom's CP bunker lit up with calls from several sectors screaming that we were firing into their trenches. We called cease fire. Fortunately no one was hit. It seems that every squad had their own "North Star." After that we went back to our old method, but instead of stopping the firing, we shifted the firing to different guns if one came under fire.

19 January 1953

Today has been fairly uneventful. I spent most of the day in the valley at battery headquarters. We're getting a new battalion commander, so everyone is hopping about. . . . Tonight, I'm sleepy from last night's guard duty, so I think I'll turn in early before my guard shift comes up tonight.

Dan's unit (C Battery) is being rotated with Cushman's platoon from his old company (D). He will be with an artillery unit near me. . . .

P.S. The naval air attack against friendly forces [you asked about in your letter] took place about Christmas and appeared in your papers on 9 January. One of Dan's gunners shot down one of the planes, and the pilot had the nerve to get mad about it when he was picked up.

20 January 1953

Today I received your letters of the 12th and 13th. . . . Your job sounds very good. . . . I believe it was worth waiting for.

The general issued an order saying everyone will have a shower at least once a week—he neglected to say how and where. Today we're building ammo bunkers. The general drove by and saw all our ammo stacked in a huge pile by the road, so we're having to build a bunker large enough to store it. It turned out to be a tremendous undertaking.

Tonight I'll be on guard duty for my two-hour relief. . . . I look up at the stars, breathe the cold night air, and think of you.

21 January 1953

Today has been a very eventful day and ended up leaving me platoon leader. Yep, your old husband has a platoon all his own, detached from the rest of the battery and operating up here in firing range of the front lines. . . . Actually, I hated to see Baker go. He and I got along very well together. . . . Since he's due to go home in another month or so, they moved him back to battery headquarters.

I'm going to make my men want to work for me . . . and do my best to make them trust me as their leader and be willing to do whatever I ask of them. [Just like Nutting, I was already becoming "rank" happy.]

The ROKs

22 January 1953

There was a language barrier between the Korean (ROK) infantry manning the front lines and their American support services. Few Koreans could speak English, and essentially no Americans could speak Korean. Two communication networks were necessary, one for the 45th Division and one for the ROK 12th Infantry Division. The main contact between the two were the artillery FOs, who were stationed at strategic observation bunkers along the ROK trenches with an interpreter. These FOs directed the fire of 45th Division artillery units and provided liaison with interpreters to coordinate the activities between the Koreans and the Americans. During an enemy attack, they kept the Americans informed of the ROK's tactical situation.

Two of the ROK infantry officers in charge of troops along our regimental front came to meet me. Neither could speak English very well. They were more interested in discussions of our hometowns than the war. When we offered them a beer from two cases stored on the ground under Baker's bunk, we found that all the beer cans were frozen solid, even though we kept the oil heater going twenty-four hours a day. The permafrost, along with nighttime temperatures of 30 degrees below zero, had overcome the hissing heater. The Koreans settled for cans of hot chocolate. The senior officer, Lieutenant Lee, seemed particularly interested in learning to speak English and learning more about the United States. I offered to help him and invited him to come back any time.

Whereas the American troops used trucks to carry and distribute all supplies, meals, etc., a good deal of the ROK supplies were carried up the hills to the trenches on the backs of Korean Service Corps personnel, usually called Choggies by the Americans. The Choggies were said to have been originally made up of three South Korean National Guard divisions. They were men who were unsuited to soldiering for various reasons, the most common being that they were too old.

Each Choggy had a carrying rack formed by an A-frame—actually a tripod with three poles of equal length, fastened together just above the head.

First Lt. Hamilton (Hamp) Davis.

Second Lt. Dudley Hughes.

Second Lt. Dan A. Hughes (left).

Building new FDC hootchie,
2nd Platoon, A Battery.

SMOKE VALLEY, JANUARY 1953

These frames were loaded with an unbelievable amount of supplies, often weighing over one hundred pounds. Two of the legs had shoulder straps about six inches below shoulder height. A little Korean would back into the straps, lean forward slightly to tilt the rear pole off the ground, then lift the other two poles, with the load, off the ground, using only leg muscles. Keeping the load level and balanced, he would move with a slow, even gait that made his legs look bowed. When stopping, he would go through the same procedure in reverse, squatting to set the front poles on the ground then leaning back until the rear pole touched. Single file, they would form a line and slowly move up steep mountain trails for hours at a time.

The Korean Service Corps had dug most of the entrenchments along the front lines. They were also the principal workers and architects who built our log and sandbag bunkers, and they were still building our gun emplacements and hootchies as requested. It was said that one man with his A-frame could carry one of the logs used in the bunker construction. It was jokingly said that if your jeep was missing it had probably been carried off on an A-frame.

23 January 1953

Yesterday a new officer was sent out for me to teach how to operate the fire direction center. He's 1st Lt. Hamilton Davis from Georgia [platoon leader of Whitlock's 1st Platoon]. As he's a "first lieutenant," it's somewhat doubtful as to just who is in charge. We get along good though—he won't be here long [I was not ready to give up my command].

Davis, nicknamed "Hamp," was from Moultrie, Georgia, and a graduate of Georgia Tech. He was a gangly, freckled-faced redhead, very talkative, with a strong southern accent. One got the impression that the "Rambling-wreck from Georgia Tech" in his college song was about him.

We are starting to build another hootchie to be used exclusively for the FDC, and move all our maps and equipment into it. . . .

I've made friends with a couple of young Korean officers that have a company of ROK infantry in the trenches adjacent to us. One [Lieutenant Lee] has been coming down regularly to visit me and take English lessons. He is very coopera-tive. Yesterday a ROK soldier stole some clothes from one squad and Lieutenant Lee got them back for us [woe unto the guy who did the stealing]. He has a great taste for the canned chocolate milk we offer him. The other day he asked if I was married, so I showed him your picture. He put on an awed expression and

Enemy lines from South Korean trenches.

Frontline trench.

Enemy trench being bombed.

Trenches on flank of Hill 854.

DAN'S FRONT LINE IN SMOKE VALLEY SECTOR

said "O, she beautiful." I asked if he was married. He replied, "No, but have girlfriend. She not look like that."

In another letter I'll tell you about Pak and Gene, our houseboys. Gene is really sharp.

Lieutenant Lee's return of the stolen clothes had been in response to a request by me. One morning I was sitting on the icy throne in the latrine with the door open, looking out down the valley, when I saw it. Above the noncom's bunker the houseboys had stretched a clothesline on which they hung the laundry of the bunker's occupants, consisting of underclothes, socks, bedding, and other items. Suddenly a Korean began quietly running down the clothesline jerking off the hanging clothes and stuffing them under his arm. He ran off with most of the clothes. I yelled and raised my carbine, but a sixth sense told me not to fire; it didn't seem worthwhile to shoot someone for stealing a few clothes. Instead, I reported the incident to Lieutenant Lee. Koreans would deal out more severe punishment than Americans, if they located the culprit. A day later most of the clothes were returned. Later in my tour, one of the American troops in another battery shot and killed a ROK seen stealing. This caused a lot of friction between the ROKs and Americans. I was glad that I hadn't shot the guy.

Second letter on 23 January, evening:

Well, how's my working girl—still dragging in the money I hope. Tonight Lieutenant Davis and I went up to the tank company and had dinner with their officers. It was quite jolly and we became well acquainted.

24 January 1953

Today was uneventful—we spent most of the day indoors working on maps. Around noon the battery commander (Whitlock) came up, and we visited some of the gun positions. Work is pretty well under way on the new FDC hootchie.

Tonight I gave Lieutenant Davis instructions on how to work the various instruments and go through the various steps in calculating indirect fire. We called out a number of missions to the guns [we were firing every night].

Gene came in and gave me a massage. He wants to be a prize-fighter when he grows up, but he has such a sharp mind that I'm encouraging him to study something else.

It was now obvious that Davis was the platoon leader, not me. Whitlock had switched platoons with Baker and Davis so that Davis could learn the indirect fire techniques we had developed, while Baker would begin to train the 1st Platoon gunners in the indirect fire procedures.

25 January 1953

Today I was never so surprised or pleased as I opened my Christmas present from you and found you smiling at me from six breathtaking positions. . . . It's hard to realize that such a beautiful creature as you exists. . . . It's the best Christmas gift I could have gotten, short of you in person. . . .

Tonight ends my fourth week since coming here to A Battery. . . . Lieutenant Davis brought out his high-powered shortwave radio. We are getting good music and programs now. The soft music and your pictures give this hootchie a very pleasant atmosphere.

(Robbie worked part-time as a model for some of the big department stores in Dallas, such as Neiman-Marcus. She had posed for six pictures using a professional model photographer for my Christmas present.)

26 January 1953

Lieutenant Whitlock is going to Inchon today to gunnery school. Today was warm enough to take pictures with no coat. Whitlock took some of my film to be developed.

Mail has been held up for the past three days, so I have nothing current to talk about. Your job sounds wonderful.

27 January 1953

Tonight my Korean friend, Lieutenant Lee, came by for a while. He's still trying to learn English, and he had a new camera that he'd traded for. Lieutenant Davis and I showed him how to use it and gave him a roll of film. He said he would come every day to learn more English. He had an album of dim yellow prints of grim-faced relatives, girlfriends, and soldiers in his unit. He was ashamed to show his girlfriends after seeing those new pictures of you, but I assured him that I thought his girls were very pretty.

Our best houseboy, Gene, acts as interpreter and keeps the conversation rolling. Gene has about the best mind of anyone I've met over here. . . . In a month he picked up English, even big words. Whereas we have to speak to most houseboys—even those who have been with American troops for years—in a broken jargon, we can talk to him as though he had lived in the US all his life. He is only seventeen years old but does the washing for the entire platoon headquarters, keeps our hootchie spotless, brings our meals, washes mess gear, gives massages, and comes running when we call.

While we were figuring out how Lieutenant Lee's camera worked, Davis and I couldn't decide what one knob was for. Gene explained its purpose. I asked

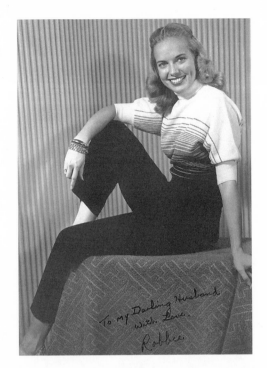

ROBBIE'S CHRISTMAS PICTURES TO DUDLEY IN KOREA

NORTH KOREAN CURRENCY TAKEN FROM A PRISONER BY LIEUTENANT LEE

Houseboy washing clothes.

"Okie" houseboy.

ROKs.

ROK on ridgeline (no-man's-land in valley).

KOREANS ON THE FRONT LINE

how he knew. He replied that he had seen this type of camera advertised in an American magazine and remembered how it was described [he had taught himself to read English too].

Pak and Gene liked American food, but not as much as they liked "kimchi," a Korean dish of blood-red cabbage that had been fermented in a broth of chili, garlic, and ginger, with a strong pungent odor. Since we were in support of the Korean infantry, the two boys often visited ROKs at mealtime, and came back with their breath reeking of the sour food. The spoken Korean language includes guttural sounds, similar to that of someone clearing their throat, "ha-r-r-r-r-r-r-k." Hamp and I would tease them, saying, "Ha-r-r-r-r-r-r-k, kimchi number ten, must be made with skunk juice." "No, kimchi number one! GI chow number ten," they would retort. I suspected the fermented cabbage generated enough alcohol to give them a slight buzz.

Periodically one of the houseboys would request a week off to return to his home. As he prepared to leave he would appear to have gained a lot of weight due to several layers of clothing he had added. He would take a bag packed with C rations and other staples. Also, he would hide all the money he had earned somewhere on his body. The American soldiers usually gave them the extra food, clothes, and some extra money to take home to their families. The boys had to hitchhike to their villages and back, but American trucks traveling to and from the rear willingly gave them rides. Their biggest problem was getting past Korean military police, who sometimes took part of their loot.

28 January 1953

Dan came over this afternoon and took pictures. Maybe the next batch Dan sends home will include a few of me—I've been missing out on all the glory. . . .

Tonight Lieutenant Lee dropped by with some information. This is secret military information, but by the time you receive this the 45th Division will have shifted to the west about ten miles. . . .

Dan said that Mother and Dad thought I was in a hot spot from my letters to you. I don't know how they could have gotten that idea. . . . I assure you that I'm as safe here as you are driving to work everyday.

29 January 1953

I just finished three hours of teaching the American language and the American way of life to our houseboys and Lieutenant Lee. I think they are impressed by the way we farm huge tracts of land by machinery with few people. Here the farms are about the size of a city block, but each one supports the entire family and labor is done painstakingly by hand. Maybe the houseboys and others like them will pull this country out of its centuries-old rut.

Tonight we got a definite fix on the enemy spotlight, but it turned out to be one of ours. . . . We should have known that the Communists wouldn't dare show us a target that tempting.

30 January 1953

They've stopped all the incoming and outgoing mail for the next five days while we move. . . . Today I went into battery headquarters to take a flu shot. I spent the rest of the day in the hootchie working out firing data for the unit relieving us. I guess that I worked at least eight hours over my maps. It seems that I work on maps no matter where I am or what my job is.

31 January 1953

After the battle for Hill 854, Dan's platoon built new positions farther back from the trench lines for four of its frontline guns. These positions were much better suited for indirect fire. He trained his platoon in the indirect fire techniques, and they became the first platoon to begin firing indirect fire in his regimental sector (the second in our battalion).

Lacking the steel azimuth bands on the turrets, he first used a white tape around the turrets marked with the azimuth scale. The battalion quickly furnished him with the marked steel bands, which they were planning to supply to all the guns. He computed the firing data in an FDC set up in his hootchie, located south of Hill 854. He commenced delivering indirect quad-50 fire within his infantry regimental sector around 18 January and soon was firing every night.

On 30 January, Dan's platoon changed places with Lieutenant Cushman's platoon, and Dan moved into his positions in the north end of Smoke Valley. These were designated as "air defense" positions around the 160th Field Artillery Battalion. This proved to be a significant move, as it was soon obvious that these positions were out of sight from the enemy but close enough to deliver indirect quad-50 fire at enemy targets both day and night without being detected. This was to set the stage for the next round of advancement in quad-50 indirect fire tactics, with the guns being located farther back. Another improvement that Dan implemented was to set up the quad-50 platoon FDC in the same large bunker as the field artillery FDC, where communications with the FOs was much better and a wider scope of all the action on the front was provided.

Lieutenant Cushman also began delivering indirect quad-50 fire from the positions he had taken over from Dan. This meant that A, C, and D Batteries were contributing to the nightly 50-caliber fire in support of the infantry.

From the time that we began firing the quad-50s in indirect fire on a regular nightly basis, the amount of incoming mortar and artillery rounds had greatly increased. Most of the shelling was at night, although indiscriminate rounds dropped from the sky at irregular intervals to harass anyone moving about during daytime.

Sequence of January events:

3 JANUARY 1953: 2nd Platoon, A Battery attempted the first indirect fire mission in 145th AAA AW Battalion.

11 JANUARY 1953: 2nd Platoon, A Battery used its quad-50s to help repulse enemy attack on Hill 854 on nights of 11 and 12 January, firing approximately 43,000 rounds, 17,900 in our western section (gun numbers 1, 2, 3, and 4) and 25,000 rounds in Sergeant Main's eastern section, three miles to the northeast (gun numbers 5, 6, 7, and 8).

21 JANUARY 1953: Lt. Col. Henry A. Cunningham Jr. departed, and Lt. Col. Everett D. Light assumed command of the 145th AAA AW Battalion.

31 JANUARY 1953: Approximate rounds fired during the month of January by the 145th AAA AW Battalion (corrected):

A Battery	241,505 rounds
B Battery	0 rounds
C Battery	40,500 rounds
D Battery	28,200 rounds
Battalion total	310,205 rounds (brass: 45,946 pounds)

FOOTNOTE: Colonel Light assumed command on 21 January and was not aware of the sequence of events. His battalion report for January did not mention the Battle for Hill 854. It stated that the first attempt at indirect fire took place on 31 January 1953. The rounds fired in the Battle for Hill 854 by Sergeant Main's guns were attributed to C Battery. Sgt. Archie Hall was reported wounded in A Battery on 31 January, when actually he was wounded on 2 February in the Battle for Hill 812. He corrected some of these errors and omissions in his February 1953 report, but it was not until his March 1953 report that he showed full awareness of the battalion's activities.

Action on the Western Front

In combat the individual soldier concentrates on killing the enemy facing him and keeping himself from becoming a casualty. He is usually not aware of the "big picture." Unbeknownst to us, on the day President Eisenhower was inaugurated, 24 January 1953, the UN forces launched a major daylight bombardment on Spud Hill, an outpost in the T-Bone area near Chorwon, some sixty miles west of our position. Several general officers and a large number of correspondents watched the action.

On the first day, a battalion of the 7th Division artillery poured thousands of rounds of 105 mm fire on the small target while the air force bombed the hill with 136,000 pounds of bombs and fourteen napalm tanks. The following day F-84 Thunderjets made numerous passes unloading thousand-pound bombs on the hill. The artillery, mortars, antiaircraft automatic weapons (ack-ack), and tanks blasted the hill. Spud Hill was then assaulted by the infantry in daylight hours. The defenders, largely unscathed, came pouring out of their caves and trenches like fire ants out of an anthill. Using light weapons and grenades, they drove back our attack, inflicting numerous casualties. Despite the two days of heavy bombardment, reports show that there were only sixty-five Chinese casualties vs. seventy-seven UN casualties. This failed major effort, with all its publicity, was between the periods of our battles, and overshadowed our success. Being in support of a ROK infantry unit, our battles attracted little coverage by the American press.

> Much of the bitter struggle of the last spring went unreported. There were months when as many as 104 enemy attacks—from company to division strength—smashed against the UN outpost line, and days when as many as 131,088 rounds of Communist artillery fell on it within a twenty-four-hour period. Few of these events, buried deep in newspapers, caused a stir. (Fehrenbach 1963, 426)

The action at Spud Hill confirmed our own experiences. Well-dug-in troops can endure prolonged, merciless shelling and bombing with negligible casualties, but troops in the open will be massacred. It seems unbelievable that during World War I hundreds of infantrymen were ordered to leave the safety of their trenches to charge the enemy trenches, only to be mowed down by machine gun and rifle fire. It is easy to see why poison gasses were used to try to destroy the enemy in their dug-in positions.

The Battle for Hill 812

1 February 1953

Today I was supposed to get paid, but I found to my dismay that I haven't turned in my pay record yet. That means I can't get paid until it is sent back to Yongdungpo. It will be March before I get any pay. Lieutenant Davis loaned me $50, which will easily carry me over.

This afternoon [officers from] the battery of the 140th AAA AW, which we are going to exchange places with, came up to look over our positions. Who should be the platoon leader of the platoon that is taking our place but Lt. Jim Moore, the Aggie who had the apartment next to John and Margie Morgan at Fort Bliss. He and I were glad to see each other. . . . [John Morgan was also an Aggie. His wife, Margie, became Robbie's close friend at Fort Bliss].

Jim was pleased with our location, but couldn't understand the complicated indirect fire system we use. I think they are going to leave me here with Jim for a few days after the platoons change places in order for me to teach them how it operates.

He said that we were being moved to an ideal location. . . . We'll be living in a BOQ with cement floor and plywood-covered interior. Imagine getting away from dirt or sandbag floors and plain log or sandbag walls.

The 140th AAA AW Battalion was a part of the 40th Infantry Division, formally a National Guard division from California and the only National Guard division other than the 45th to see combat in the Korean War. It was also part of the X Corps.

2 February 1953

Mail started up again today and I got your letters of 22, 26, and 27 January. . . . Thanks for the mantles.

On 2 February the 37th Regiment of the ROK 12th Division reported enemy troops concentrating at Luke's Castle for an attack on Hill 812. This hill was 4,000 yards north of the four guns near our platoon CP and 2,000 yards northwest of Sergeant Main's four guns. As mentioned previously, an attack had failed against Hill 812 six weeks earlier, on Christmas day.

Shells began exploding all around our positions late that night, a repeat of the previous attack. We were ready this time. Hill 812 was inside our lines, but on the southeast end of a ridge that trended upward toward the enemy trenches. Higher up the ridge, a prominent rock outcrop (Luke's Castle) was behind the Communist lines. Our field artillery poured intense fire into the assembly area around Luke's Castle. This didn't stop them. Around midnight, a North Korean battalion (more than seven hundred men) charged down the ridge toward our fortifications on Hill 812. The field artillery FO called for quad-50 fire to create a wall of fire across the ridge. Our eight guns were in perfect position to systematically saturate the area. The attackers suddenly found themselves in a hail of 50-caliber bullets flashing over the ground in their path. They took their hits and charged on anyway. During the action Lt. Hamilton (Hamp) Davis handled the telephone while I calculated the settings for the guns. Outside our bunker, the night air reverberated with constant bombardments from enemy mortar and artillery, but we were too busy to worry about it.

Dan's platoon (having changed positions with Cushman's platoon) was located at the north end of Smoke Valley, south of Sergeant Main's guns. Although his main mission was to provide air defense, he had also been providing quad-50 indirect fire for the ROK regiment to which he was attached. This new innovation in the use of quad-50s, located farther back from the front lines to provide indirect fire, would change our tactical deployment of the tracks in the near future. Since Dan was in a different regimental sector, there was no direct telephone line to my platoon. He had to ring from his platoon to his battery, then to battalion, then to the A Battery CP, then up to my platoon—five switchboards altogether.

Our switchboard signaled that my brother was on a line. Dan's voice asked, "What's happening?"

"The gooks are attacking Hill 812 from Luke's Castle."

"I think I can reach that ridge with my guns here in Smoke Valley. Give me some of the targets."

Hamp gave him coordinates to the main targets. Soon he had several guns firing to strengthen the wall of fire. One of Dan's men was wounded by mortar fragments.

About an hour into the battle, our first sergeant sprinted 40 feet through the gauntlet of explosions from the enlisted men's CP bunker, suddenly appearing through our door. He shouted, "The number two gun has been hit and is out of action." A mortar round had hit at the side of the halftrack and blew the gunner out of the turret. Sgt. Archie Hall, the gunner, was wounded by shell fragments in his abdomen and about his face. His flak jacket stopped much of the shrapnel and probably saved his life. Our medic, a corporal who usually lounged around with nothing to do, tore out through the exploding shells for a 150-yard run to the crippled halftrack. He administered medical aid to Sergeant Hall for several hours until an ambulance was able to come up once the shelling had subsided. The gunner was evacuated to a hospital ship after treatment at the division hospital. We never heard from him afterward. (The medic was later awarded a Bronze Star for valor.)

The North Koreans fought their way down the ridge. Within 50 yards of the ROK positions, a hand grenade battle broke out that lasted for some time and pinned down the attackers. The artillery forward observer reported to his battalion S-2 that the enemy had taken Hill 812 at 0335 hours. A reinforced ROK company counterattacked and retook the hill ten minutes later. The North Koreans had to retreat, again through the 50-caliber curtain of fire, to reach the safety of their lines.

Eventually, the firing tapered off and we breathed sighs of relief. It was hard to believe we had come through with only one serious casualty in our platoon. We were given the order to cease fire. When the shooting finally ended it was almost daylight (see Maps 7 and 8).

Lieutenant Whitlock showed up, demanding of Hamp, "Why didn't you go out to check on the wounded man?" "Sir, we couldn't leave our post. Who would direct the fire for the guns if more ack-ack was called for?" Whitlock was not satisfied with the answer, but I sided with Hamp. The use of quad-50s in indirect fire had changed priorities. The quad-50 fire was proving to be an indispensable part of regimental firepower.

The S-3 of the 145th AAA AW Battalion delivered this report on 3 February 1953:

Btry A participated in repulsing an est. Bn sized attack on Hill 812. 36,000 rounds fired. [Additional rounds fired by Dan's platoon were not in the report.]

Information was also furnished in a report on the action written by Walter G. Hermes:

On the night of 2 February, the 37th Regiment of the ROK 12th Division reported enemy troops concentrating for an attack. Intense artillery fire

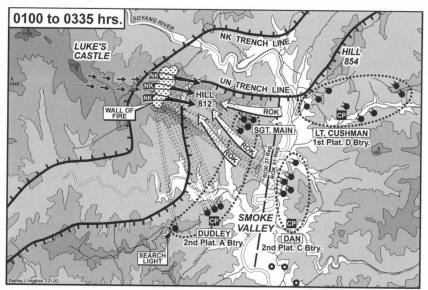

Map #7 Early morning on 3 February 1953, a battalion of North Korean troops attacked Hill 812 (37th Regiment of the ROK 12th Division) from Luke's Castle. Quad-50 machine gun fire from the 2nd Platoon, A Battery (Dudley) and 2nd Platoon, C Battery (Dan) placed a wall of fire in the path of the attacking force.

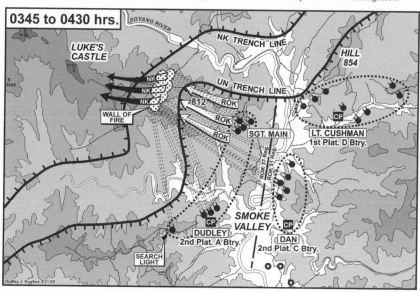

Map #8 A counterattack by ROK forces drove them back at 0345 hrs. The attackers had to retreat through the wall of fire.

MAPS 7 AND 8 ROLE OF THE ACK-ACK IN THE BATTLE FOR HILL 812

171st Field Artillery Battalion headquarters.

171st FA FDC. Shared with Dan's FDC, C Battery, 145th AAA AW Battalion, January to February.

Prepare to fire.

Quad-50 in direct fire position.

SMOKE VALLEY, JANUARY 1953

poured into the assembly area, but a North Korean battalion pushed on towards the hill [812]. Within fifty yards of the ROK positions, a savage grenade battle broke out and lasted until a reinforcing ROK company turned the tide. The North Koreans used close to 7,000 rounds of mixed explosive ammunition in this heaviest action of the month, and suffered over a hundred estimated casualties. They received over twice as many rounds from UNC artillery. (Hermes 1966, 377)

3 February 1953

The last twenty-four hours have been quite a strain. . . . I'm going to have to hit the sack pretty quick to catch up on my sleep. We've been really working for the last few hours.

My battery is getting a commendation from the commanding general of the X Corps for the excellent firing my platoon has done [for helping to repel a large-scale enemy attack on 12 January]. I have an idea that more honors will be bestowed upon us shortly.

In two days we'll move back and live a life of relaxation and ease. I've forgotten what a movie is like. . . . Also, if I start taking a daily shower I doubt that my skin can stand the strain—once it wears down to the skin.

When the coffee gets here it will really be appreciated. Lieutenant Davis has a coffee pot. His houseboy is a #1 coffee maker. Each morning his houseboy wakes me by handing me a cup of hot coffee. . . .

This experience over here is really making a man of me. . . . Your prayers help.

4 February 1953

I got a good night's sleep last night. This morning the package you mailed on December 1st arrived. The cookies were ruined, but the candy came through in fine shape. I had a breakfast of fudge and coffee. . . .

It looks like it will be a fairly warm day here. It may be warm enough to snow. I hope it holds off snowing until we get the tracks out tomorrow.

5 February 1953

During this cold, sunny day, I was walking from the position of gun #1 back to our hootchie along the road on the reverse slope of the ridge. The road was surfaced with crushed pink granite, courtesy of the engineers. Suddenly there came the s-h-u-s-h—s-h-u-s-h—s-h-u-s-h whisper of an incoming mortar round. I threw myself flat on the road only to hear a THUD. The shell had landed about 20 feet away but failed to explode. Two more rounds followed the first: s-h-u-s-h THUD, s-h-u-s-h THUD. Three shells were all duds. It seemed incredible that all three failed to explode. Was this divine intervention or just bad ammunition? In either case, I was grateful. They say you never hear the one that gets you, but I question that, too.

I was not completely unscathed, however. When I hit the road my chin landed on a chunk of the granite. My lower lip was badly cut and my lower teeth loosened. After getting back to platoon headquarters, the medic dressed my lip and said he would recommend me for a Purple Heart.

"Like hell you will. This is self-inflicted, not caused by being hit. Forget that!" I could picture my wife getting a notice that I was "wounded in battle." In my letters to Robbie, I was careful to play down any danger from combat. My letters sounded like I was on a Boy Scout camping trip, having fun.

He said "Okay, if that's the way you want it."

Other incidents of Communist shells failing to explode were common. The field artillery FO, who directed the quad-50 fire in C Battery, had been in Smoke Valley when it was bombed by friendly planes. He was very nervous after that. A few weeks later he was directing quad-50 fire from his FO bunker on the front line. His view of the battlefield was a horizontal slit about 8 inches high and 36 inches long. He was looking out of the slit with field glasses when a 76 mm artillery shell came through the slit, hit the wall behind him, bounced to the floor, and then rolled under his bunk. The shell had barely missed him and didn't explode. He was so shook up that he became hysterical and had to be relieved.

Another 76 mm round came through the radiator of one of Dan's half-tracks. The radiator was protected by strips of armor that worked like a venetian blind, but they were in the open position. The round buried itself in the engine block but failed to explode. These failures were probably from old World War II munitions.

The ROKs began to bring in a number of prisoners. We believed these were mostly deserters who wanted to escape from the suicidal mentality of their commanders. Surrender leaflets had been scattered along the trenches by canister shells from both sides and by air drops from UN planes. The South Koreans were not fooled by the propaganda leaflets, which were numerous in our countryside, some showing their wives and sisters being raped by American soldiers. On quiet nights the Communists used loud-speakers to play Korean music and spouted propaganda in Korean to the

ROK infantry. We learned from surrendering Communists that they had been told that the Americans tortured and shot all prisoners, making them apprehensive of surrender. They surrendered only out of desperation, waving their surrender leaflets and hoping we would honor them.

6 February 1953

My platoon moved out yesterday, so for the past couple of days I've been working with Jim Moore and his platoon to get them ready to fire. Tomorrow a jeep will come for me to carry me back to our new area to join the platoon. I've really worked hard and with very little sleep the past couple of days, but I believe Jim is going to be in pretty good shape by the time I leave tomorrow.

I think the first thing I'll do when I get to the new area is to take a hot shower, put on clean clothes, then go to the mess hall and eat a meal off of a plate on a table instead of a mess kit balanced on my knee. Next I'll go to a movie. Then at night I can go to bed and dream of you without having to jump out of bed to calculate fire missions for the bigger part of the night. . . .

I've got an awfully sore lip. I hit my mouth on a rock and busted my lip pretty badly a couple of days ago. It's much better now and I think it'll be OK in a few days.

Tonight Jim and I have been talking about how nice it would be to be home with our wives. He's been away from home for nine months, and the three months I've been away seems like a lifetime. . . . It's going to be so nice to be with you again that I just can't imagine it in my present environment.

Apparently, the 40th Division quickly became efficient in the quad-50 indirect fire technique. One of their infantrymen with the 223rd Regiment, Victor Spaulding, referred to their use of it in the spring of 1953. Spaulding arrived in Korea in time to be on line during the last three months of combat:

> One of the most frightening moments up on Heartbreak Ridge was when we had quad-50s set up for indirect fire. . . . I began to see what I thought was muzzle fire at us. One of our patrols [had] picked up sounds indicating the Chinese were approaching our lines. They called for the 50-caliber machine guns to give them indirect fire. When the armor-piercing bullets hit the ground, they would explode and become anti-personnel weapons. . . . What I was seeing were the bursts. (Pruitt 2002, 311)

The Move to Heartbreak Ridge

I was not particularly sorry to be leaving our high mountain area in view of the action we had been exposed to during the last few weeks. I had been on the front line for forty days, which seemed more like forty weeks. Looking back, this 40 days was probably the highlight of my Korean combat experience.

A Battery of the 145th AAA AW Battalion received a commendation from Lt. Gen. I. D. White, commander of the X Corps, in recognition of our part in repelling the enemy attack on Hill 852 on 12 January 1953 using massed quad-50 machine gun fire (only my platoon was doing the firing).

Later, when my tour was completed, I was presented a Bronze Star for "meritorious service" with citation, a portion of which stated:

> Lieutenant HUGHES was assigned responsibility for coordinating an antiaircraft fire direction center with a field artillery battalion. Procedures which he worked out for indirect fire were new and entailed complete training of his platoon in methods never used before. While supporting infantry units, Lieutenant HUGHES devoted himself with untiring vigor and enthusiasm to making the fire of his platoon highly effective and efficient, and as a result contributed greatly to the repulsing of several large enemy attacks.

7 February 1953

My jeep picked me up on the morning of 7 February and drove me to the rear, several miles past the old battalion headquarters. From there we drove westward for a few miles to another river valley, then northward toward the front lines. My platoon's new location was on the west side of Heartbreak Ridge (about ten miles west of our previous position in Smoke Valley). As we drove northward, we passed several units of field artillery that were strung out down the valley. Several miles from the front were a few 155 mm Long Toms and eight-inch howitzers. Farther up the valley were battalions of 105 mm and 155 mm howitzers. Nearest to the front line were 105 mm howitzers. Finally, we arrived at the location of the northernmost 105 mm battalion.

Our platoon CP was located within the 158th Field Artillery Battalion, about 2,500 yards behind the MLR. That location provided the advantage of mess halls, showers, and other conveniences. The immediate mission of my platoon was to provide air defense for the 158th Field Artillery Battalion. Our new location was in the Mundung-ni Valley ("-ni"or "-ri" means "village" in Korean); however, the hamlet of Mundung-ni was in enemy territory to the north. Therefore, the 145th Battalion Headquarters referred to our location as Worun-ni, more commonly called the Heartbreak Ridge sector. A river called the Slip-chon ("-chon" is one of the Korean words for river) ran south, down the Mundung-ni Valley.

Dan's platoon was situated adjacent to mine in the Sat'ae-ri Valley east of Heartbreak Ridge, where a parallel river called the So-chon flowed south. His guns were positioned to give ground fire along an approximately four-mile front, in support of the 180th Infantry Regiment of the 45th Division. He had been firing missions every night, again operating from the 171st Field Artillery FDC in his valley. It was a relief to have American infantry. No interpreters were needed; everyone spoke English.

Our platoon had only four halftracks situated around the 158th Field Artillery Battalion, the other four having been sent back to the 45th Division airstrip. My first few days would be spent positioning the guns.

As we approached our new location, we passed a number of large bunkers, one of which was the 158th Field Artilllery FDC. Others contained the officers' mess, headquarters for the 158th Field Artillery Battalion, and, near the top of the valley, our 2nd Platoon, A Battery CP. Up a flight of steps, about 20 feet above the CP bunker was the BOQ bunker, where Hamp and I were quartered. This hootchie was somewhat smaller than our former one. It had a concrete floor and plywood paneling, with no windows except a small glass panel in the door.

The officers' mess was conveniently located just down the hill from our quarters. Dinner was served early since most of the firing occurred at night. Immediately inside the door of the mess bunker was a small but well-stocked bar, which was manned by Monroe, an older warrant officer who had been a bartender in New York. His speciality was a Manhattan. I had never tasted a Manhattan before, but I liked its bittersweet taste. Time would reveal that Monroe had duties other than bartending each evening. He carefully gauged the amount each officer drank, usually limiting each to two drinks. Strangely enough, wine was seldom available, except for fortified wines, such as port and sherry. It seems that wine spoils if it is exposed to temperatures below 25 degrees F or above 95 degrees F. With the bitter cold winters and the hot summers, it was too difficult to transport to the front lines in drinkable condition.

Being the 158th Field Artillery Battalion officers' mess, those attending were mostly field artillerymen. There were six or eight lieutenants, with several captains, majors, and two light (lieutenant) colonels. Also, there was an air force first lieutenant who was ground coordinator for air strikes along our front.

The dress was more military than it had been when we were isolated on the front line in support of the ROKs. Everyone shaved, and uniforms were neat and clean. An officers' sandbagged shower tent was available with enough water for each of us to shower at least once a week. The artillery battalion commanding officer, a lieutenant colonel, sat at the head of the table, with the other officers seated by rank down either side. Being the lowest officer on the totem pole, I was seated at the far end, nearest the door. The mess bunker was sturdy enough to withstand the shelling that took place periodically, day and night.

Captain Boone, a doctor from the medical corps, was assigned to the artillery battalion as medical officer. I learned he was popular for his stories of sexual incidents associated with his civilian practice. This particular evening, Captain Boone casually related a story about being shelled earlier in the afternoon. His quarters were in a BOQ bunker just adjacent to this officers' mess bunker. Only a ten-inch space separated the two adjacent walls of sandbags between the bunkers. Boone was determined to live to renew his practice in the States, including his sexual escapades, when his tour of duty was over. For that reason, he never went outdoors except when absolutely necessary. That was mostly for sick call each morning, toilet, and meals. His bunk, which he occupied most of the time, was next to the wall closest to the mess hall. He had added shelves over his bunk to set up a medical library on the wall.

That afternoon he was lying in his bunk reading when there was a muffled explosion. The medical volumes were suddenly jarred out of the shelves and covered him. He pushed them aside then went outside to see what had happened. He found that what he believed to be a mortar round had dropped into the ten-inch space between the walls and exploded within two feet of his head on the outside of the bunker. This incident only strengthened his resolve to stay indoors. (Most of the incoming rounds were artillery, as our hootchies were near maximum range for mortars.)

For the next two days, I had to get the gun positions in shape. Hamp had gone to the airstrip with four of the platoon's squads, then on to the gunnery school in Inchon with them, leaving me the job of getting our guns in position around the 158th Field Artillery as well as the airstrip. I was able to get a shower, but had yet to take in a movie.

During our stay on the front, all shaving and washing was from water in a steel helmet. Our main attempt at physical hygiene was to change our wool long-handles weekly so they could be washed by the houseboys. Otherwise, I had worn the same clothes for the forty days on line, as had everyone else. Strangely, in the extremely cold weather no one felt the need to bathe. In the shower, the warm water was almost a forgotten sensation. To conserve water, it was turned off while one lathered up, then turned back on to rinse the soap off. It took three soaps to begin to feel clean.

Lieutenant Baker, now platoon leader of the 1st Platoon of A Battery, had three of his guns in direct fire positions dug in with the American troops on the front line. He did not seem to have the FDC operators necessary to conduct indirect fire. The battalion had begun to distinguish between gun positions as direct fire, indirect fire, or air defense.

With the great impact of our quad-50 indirect fire during the battles for Hills 854 and 812, the X Corps commander wanted this increase in firepower to be available to other infantry units within the X Corps. This would include the ROK 7th Infantry Division, the 5th Regimental Combat Team (RCT), and the US 40th Infantry Division. I had been held over in Smoke Valley to work with Lt. Jim Moore to teach him the indirect fire technique. His platoon became the means of introducing the system to the other three batteries of the 140th AAA AW Battalion, 40th Infantry Division.

To add quad-50 firepower to the ROK 7th Infantry Division, a platoon from B Battery of our battalion was attached to the ROK 7th Division. This was the most westerly divisional unit of the X Corps. Similarly, a platoon of quad-50s from D Battery was stationed in ground support with the 5th RCT in the Punchbowl area. The other platoon of D Battery was also stationed in the Punchbowl in AAA defense of the 160th and 555th Field Artillery Battalions. The quad-50s of the 5th RCT were attached to the 145th AAA AW to add firepower to the D Battery guns in ground support and to learn the indirect firing procedures (see Map 9, p. 120). Infantry units of the 5th RCT were scheduled to be replaced by the ROK 20th Infantry Division during the first week in March.

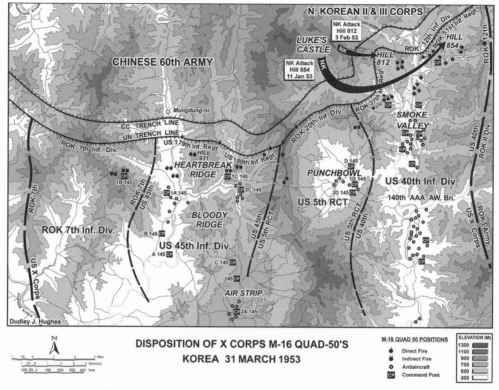

DISPOSITION OF X CORPS M-16 QUAD-50'S
KOREA 31 MARCH 1953

M-16 QUAD 50 POSITIONS	
●	Direct Fire
♦	Indirect Fire
○	Antiaircraft
CP	Command Post

ELEVATION (M)	
1300	
1100	
900	
700	
500	
300	

Map #9 Area held by the X Corp's four divisions, 31 March 1953. M-16 positions of the US 45th and US 40th Infantry Divisions are indicated. Direct fire M-16s are in bunkers along the trench lines with the infantry. Indirect fire M-16s are located in defiladed positions about 2,000 yards behind the front lines, capable of delivering indirect fire on enemy targets in daylight or nighttime operations. Antiaircraft defense M-16s are located primarily around field artillery in valleys to the rear.

The U.S. 45th Division's 145th AAA AW Battalion, being the most advanced AAA AW unit in the X Corps in the use of quad-50s in the indirect fire technique, reduced its role in air defense in order to put more of its M-16s in indirect fire positions.

Four quad-50s of B Battery (145th AAA AW) were stationed in indirect firing positions with the ROK 7th Infantry Division to the west of Heartbreak Ridge. The M-16s of D Battery, were stationed in the Punchbowl with three guns in direct firing positions dug in on line with the ROK 20th Infantry Division, four guns in indirect fire positions, and six in antiaircraft defense positions with the US 5th RCT's 555th Field Artillery Battalion.

Note: The 40th Infantry Division changed places with the 45th Infantry Division 5 February 1953 after the 45th participated in battles for Hill 854 and Hill 812

MAP 9 TENTH (X) CORPS OF THE 8TH ARMY, 31 MARCH 1953

Quad-50 squads moving out.

South view of Mungdung-ni Valley.

Icy road.

Road march, Dan's platoon, Smoke Valley to Heartbreak Ridge.

CHANGING POSITIONS, EARLY FEBRUARY 1953

The purpose of these changes was to expand quad-50 indirect fire capabilities to the entire X Corps front, rather than limiting it to the 45th Division. There was little doubt that the quad-50 fire was having great demoralizing effect on the enemy infantry and discouraging new large attacks. By now, half of the quad-50 halftracks in the 145th AAA AW Battalion were in positions to add ground fire support to the infantry, either in direct fire or indirect fire positions. This would soon be true of other antiaircraft automatic weapons units in the X Corps.

9 February 1953

I haven't been able to write for the past two days because I've worked up until midnight every day since I arrived in this new area. . . . Lieutenant Davis had been sent to Inchon to antiaircraft school there, leaving me the job of getting the platoon settled down. Here the platoon is spread out about twelve miles and it runs me ragged to get everything done. . . . [Some of the tracks were at the airstrip, while others were with the 158th Field Artillery at Heartbreak Ridge.]

10 February 1953

Today I got back the first pictures that Baker and I took. . . . These pictures were taken early before I lost weight. By the time I left the other area, I was down to 160 pounds. Here in AAA positions with three square meals a day, I will probably gain some back.

Lieutenant Davis got back tonight. Maybe I can take it easy for awhile. Tonight it's snowing softly. I went to the movie and saw Thunderbird, *a movie about the 45th Division during the last war. Now we're listening to music on Davis's radio.*

11 February 1953

Tonight I received the wallet-size pictures of you, and they are excellent, especially the one in the bathing suit. You are a wonderful wife and smart to keep us in such good financial shape. . . .

That piece in the Oak Cliff Tribune *about me took me by surprise, but I feel honored. The only part I didn't like was giving out your address. . . .*

Well, life is getting easier every day. I've now got an air mattress on my canvas cot. The food here is very good. My main jobs are supply records, inspections, communications, and other minor details.

12 February 1953

There is a rumor that I'll be sent back to the airstrip in a week or so. My platoon deserves a rest. . . . Sorry I forgot Valentine's Day. I received yours and it smells as sweet as you. I'll put one in the mail today, if I can find one at the PX.

Lieutenant Whitlock invited his officers to stop by battery headquarters for drinks. Everyone accepted, and soon we were drinking his scotch and eating tidbits he provided. Baker told me this was usually a weekly affair when things were quiet. Most of us were fresh out of college and were telling college-style jokes, which seemed funnier as the party progressed. Soon we were singing college songs led by Hamp's "Rambling Wreck from Georgia Tech" and eventually the "Aggie War Hymn." On the front line, with the daily shelling, everyone built up tension. Sessions like this offered short periods of relaxation.

13 February 1953

Today is a mild, cloudy day and may be above freezing. A blanket of gray clouds seems to be resting on the peaks of the mountains. . . . Unlike the area we were first in, there is very little vegetation on these hills. Every valley contains a swift mountain stream, and, believe it or not, they are all frozen—waterfalls, rapids, and all—one solid chunk of ice. . . .

The food here is excellent. I'm eating with headquarters battery of the 158th Field Artillery Battalion, and they live like kings. It's not yet 10:00 AM and I'm waiting for lunch—I didn't quite make it up for breakfast this morning. Lieutenant Davis went to the airstrip this morning to place some of our tracks in position.

The Airstrip

14 February 1953

Part of my platoon was to be given a break after being deeply involved in the heavy action on the line in Smoke Valley. Four tracks had been sent to the rear to guard the 45th Division Airstrip A-14 at Tokkol-li. This was a small airfield about ten miles to the rear of Heartbreak Ridge. It was still in the combat zone, but beyond the range of enemy artillery. The airstrip was used mainly for single-engine artillery spotter planes, helicopters, and small aircraft bringing in high-ranking officers.

For our four guns we had an acting platoon sergeant, Sergeant Byrd. I became the platoon leader at the airstrip. This was a three-point area.

15 February 1953

Today I was moved back to the division airstrip, way back from the front. It's so far back that I don't even have to wear a steel helmet. I feel lightheaded with nothing but a pile cap on.

I am in a BOQ tent with five airfield officers. The tent has a wooden floor and two big oil stoves that keep it quite warm. We even have electric lights. Next door is a mess hall with chairs, tables, and waiters. Out back is a shower tent with plenty of hot water. There's even a heater in the latrine. Every night there is a movie, but tonight is a Protestant service, being Sunday.

I'm the officer alone in charge here of four halftracks and their squads. Lieutenant Davis stayed with the other four back guns in the area I left. This is my best deal yet. . . . Dan is not far from here, so I think he may get over to see me sometimes. . . . There's a lot of work to be done for the next few days—after that I'll have more time to loaf. . . . P.S. The coffee got here a few days ago and we are enjoying it.

The halftracks occupied positions that had been prepared by previous occupants in the low hills around the airfield. We set up platoon headquarters in a bunker in the hills. That night I went to the officers' mess, where a bar had been set up, and met some of the other officers, including pilots. Since we didn't have to worry about running the FDC that night, we were free to drink. The bartender suggested a tawny port bottled in Scotland, which seemed to fill a gastronomical need developed from a diet of C rations. We had more with dinner. The next morning, looking in the mirror to shave, I thought my teeth were bleeding. The tawny port had stained them red. That night I complained to the bartender.

"That tawny port stained my teeth red."

"You need to decant it."

"What's that?"

He sighed at my ignorance, but explained the procedure.

16 February 1953

Sure enjoying life here at the airstrip. This is too good to last I'm afraid—but I may as well enjoy it while I can.

17 February 1953

This morning the colonel inspected my tracks around the airstrip. I believe we came out OK. . . .

Tonight I'm going to try to attend the movie right next door. . . . Also, I am going over for a shower beforehand. I've been looking for Dan to arrive to talk over oil deals.

I've got three trips to look forward to. First is a trip to Inchon for four days at AAA school beginning the 27th of February. Second is R&R to Japan around the last of April, and third, a trip home in early August. Now they are sending lots of troops home straight from Inchon by ship—that's what I'm going to try for.

Two of the officers here in my BOQ are leaving for home tomorrow. I'm enviously watching them pack.

Later: *I saw the movie, although I missed the first part because I had to check on the field phones to my tracks. It was a sword fight adventure about kings and girls.*

18 February 1953

Your last letter asked about smoking, drinking, and issue of beer to troops. My habits are about the same as when I left home. We get free cigarettes, which I never smoke, but I give them away. Cigars are available at the PX, but I seldom smoke one. The army issues free beer to all troops except in this division (45th). The general had it stopped. About once a month the PX gets beer, but it's all gone in one night. The enlisted men get very little to drink. But in a hard-working outfit like ours, there's not enough idleness to cause any complaint. It's in units where the troops have lots of time to lie around with little to do that liquor is in demand. Officers have little restriction. In every BOQ beer and whiskey are usually available to everyone in the BOQ. Most officers here are moderate drinkers, and many don't drink at all. Each officer gets three bottles of whiskey a month. I give mine to the older sergeants in the battery to distribute as they see fit. You may think that I shouldn't do this, but I found that otherwise they are tempted to drink poisonous Korean whiskey or home brew.

All in all I've seen less drinking here than at Fort Bliss. . . . I haven't changed a bit except I'm in much better physical shape.

19 February 1953

My day for going to Inchon has been changed to 23 February, returning on the 27th. I'll be the officer in charge of men from our battalion going through a three-day school.

That day was spent making a visit to each of our gun positions. These were isolated at various locations in the hills, well away from the traffic and bustle around the airport. The guns were left in position, since any attack would come from the air. Even though the odds of an air attack were probably less than a thousand to one, my assessment of the defense was that we needed one gun at the airstrip as protection from dive bombers. I chose a location for the halftrack near the end of the runway in an old rice paddy. It was near a major road that carried a lot of traffic and had hundreds of telephone lines strung on poles alongside. At my request, the engineers agreed to excavate a gun emplacement for me.

The following morning they had a tankdozer attempting to scrape an excavation in the rice paddy to give protection to the halftrack. But the ground was frozen with permafrost extending many feet into the subsurface. After making no progress over several hours, the tankdozer left. The engineers returned the next day and planted several large charges in the ground. When they exploded, tons of frozen ground were blown into the air. Traffic was stalled on the major road. Some of these chunks fell on the telephone lines, severing most of them. Soon an army of telephone repairmen from different units were working on the wires, trying to restore communications.

Eventually a major from my battalion headquarters arrived. He introduced himself and in a very cordial voice said: "Lieutenant Hughes, we appreciate your effort to set up a proper defense around this airstrip. However, we must be practical. That road is very busy, and communications have been disrupted to almost every unit for miles around. If you put a gun there, maintenance will be a problem from the dusty road. The gun crews will be under scrutiny all the time. We haven't had an air attack for over two years and don't expect any now. I would suggest that you put the gun back up in the hills out of the way and enjoy your stay here."

I felt rather foolish. "Yes sir, of course you are right."

It took a while to live this down at the officers' mess.

20 February 1953

There's a USO show going on right now, but rather than standing out in the cold to watch other girls, I decided to enjoy sitting here by the warm fire and thinking of you.

It's now right after lunch, and since most of my men are at the show, there's not much to do until they get back. Lunch today was very good, as it always is here at the airstrip. Being Friday, the main dish was fish, but well prepared.

Since my platoon was split, I had to leave Gene with the platoon command post. Here, I was assigned another houseboy called "Abbie." He's a good houseboy, but not as good as Gene.

Two women officers had chow in the officers' mess today, and of course, were the center of attention. There were over twenty officers eating and all trying to keep up a conversation with the girls. However, they held little attraction for me as I couldn't help but compare them to you.

Later: Tonight I saw a good sexy movie with Errol Flynn and Rhonda Fleming, with lots of necking and sword fighting. . . . I could picture you in her place and me in his in the passionate scenes.

21 February 1953

Besides tawny port, hot meals, and showers, there were movies every night. The houseboys never missed a movie. They were enthralled with the American way of life, which the movies revealed. Most of the officers also attended the "picture show," sitting in a reserved officers' section.

The houseboys wanted to show me the way Koreans lived. At one end of the rice paddy was a Korean farmhouse, from which the residents had been evacuated when the MLR was established. It was now occupied by several older Korean service troops whom the houseboys had befriended. The walls of the house were of stone, plaster, and hand-hewn timbers. The roof was tile. Apparently the entire social life within the house revolved around its floor, which was built from flat stones (or tile), with a crawl space underneath. A fire was built under the house using wood or coal as fuel, which heated the stone floor. Occupants lounged near the floor. They sat on pads and slept on mats with blankets to capture the heat radiating from the floor. It was not necessary to heat the space inside the house to the ceiling, only the floor. That took much less fuel. The inside of the house smelled of a hundred years or more of smoke—a strong but not unpleasant odor. A clay brazier with hot coals acted as a stove for cooking. I could see that a family could be quite cozy in the house through the coldest of weather. This grassroots view of Korean life gave me a feeling of respect toward the generations that had lived there.

22 February 1953

I've called off my usual inspection of the tracks, and instead, I'm going to write you. . . . Early tomorrow morning I'm going to Inchon. We'll leave about six o'clock in the morning and arrive there about three in the afternoon. The next two days the men will go to school, and on Thursday I'll bring them back.

Yesterday, I came out very good on inspection. These tracks around the airport are probably in the best shape of any in the battalion. . . .

Evening the same day: Tonight I went to chapel services. . . . This afternoon I took a shower and there was a large mirror in a position to get a good view of myself (such vanity). I was surprised at the trim, well-developed build I've acquired from my strenuous weeks up on the line. Even after two weeks of good chow and soft living, I'm in better shape than when I was in college.

The duties required to operate the platoon were minimal. I had time to catch up on my sleep, write letters, and read. On the front lines we were under continuous stress, night and day. It was only after relaxing in the safety and quiet of rear areas such as this that I realized how much tension we had been under. One day faded into another.

23 February 1953

Even though the distance to Inchon was only about 150 miles, at 30 miles per hour on a two-lane winding road, the trip took over six hours. We passed through many villages, plus the larger cities of Chunchon, Seoul, and Yongdungpo. At Inchon we were given quarters near Kimpo Air Base. This was one of the major airfields in the Korean air war. Flights of saber jets and other UN planes were continually taking off on missions or returning from them.

24 February 1953

Today I am in Inchon at the EUSAK AA Camp. I arrived yesterday after an all-day truck ride. Now I can enjoy a leisurely day while the men I brought are going through the school.

This morning I went to the Inchon PX and left my watch to be fixed. . . . The officers here are very friendly and we talked for hours last night. Lieutenant Herndon from Carolina is from our battery [A] but has been attached to this school for the past few months. Tonight we have a USO show at the theater, which we plan to see. . . .

Many of the ships out in Inchon Bay are returning to the US with a load of troops. I hope this is the port that I will be leaving from.

A few miles from Kimpo, a row of guns were parked about 50 yards apart along a cliff looking out over a barren stretch of water in Inchon Bay. The next morning we reported there, and the school instructors gave the

Inchon Bay.

Firing at towed target.

QUAD-50 AIR DEFENSE TRAINING, INCHON BAY, FEBRUARY 1953

squads a short refresher course in antiaircraft automatic weapon gunnery. Thereafter, the day was spent firing at targets being towed by small planes. Late in the afternoon we returned to Kimpo for another night in Inchon. Each night at Inchon I spent the evening in the officers' club, but most of the enlisted men took in the bars and other pleasures of the area.

26 February 1953

I'm back at the airstrip—my trip to Inchon is over. I'm beat after riding a bouncing truck across the Korean peninsula. We left Inchon early this morning and didn't arrive here until late in the afternoon. Our route took us from Inchon to Yongdungpo, to Seoul, to Chunchon, and finally here. The battery moved two more of my tracks down here to the airstrip while I was gone. The section leaders tell me that the colonel inspected our unit and was pleased. . . .

In Seoul we stopped at the PX to buy articles that we cannot get here. Also, in one of the Korean shops I bought a charcoal iron for pressing clothes. It has a little chamber for hot charcoal and a little chimney, quite a novelty. With this iron, I'll be one of the sharpest men in the battalion and "rise to the top," contrary to my usual slovenly appearance. . . .

As always, I was true to you in Inchon—the Korean gals didn't turn my head, and even the USO show girls didn't catch my eye. You are the only one in the world for me.

27 February 1953

Lieutenant Davis and the rest of the platoon moved down to the airstrip today. . . . Tonight I'm staying in the BOQ. . . . I talked to Dan today. He is in the Fire Direction Center of a field artillery battalion.

Locating the AAA FDC in with the FA FDC was to become standard procedure.

28 February 1953

Our detachment had arrived back at the airfield on the 26th of February. The gun crews took up their positions around the airfield, and we resumed our uneventful guard duty. A couple of days later I decided to make an inspection tour of the squads. Since I had plenty of time and needed the exercise, I decided to walk. The first position was somewhat in disarray with the men half dressed and equipment lying around. After some mild rebukes I went on to the second gun position. This one was shipshape—everyone was properly dressed with everything in order. No doubt the first squad visited had called ahead to warn the others I was coming, as that was the case with the third squad also.

The road to the fourth squad passed their quad-50 halftrack before it curved on down to the squad bunker. I inspected the halftrack first. Everything seemed in order in the rear. The ammunition canisters were full and the guns pointed skyward. A gunner could climb into the turret, flip the switch, and engage an enemy plane within seconds. As an afterthought, I opened the door to the driver's cab and was startled to see a Korean houseboy sitting in the passenger seat. He gave me a big smile, showing a perfect set of white teeth, his full lips and facial features looking almost too perfect. His hair had been cut short, in GI fashion. I asked who he was. In broken English, a soft high-pitched voice said, "Me new houseboy name Ling." Walking on down to the squad quarters, I found everything was in perfect order there. No doubt they had been warned of my visit. On my questioning, Sergeant Gonzales explained that the new houseboy was replacing the one who had left due to illness at home. Without further questions, I went on to inspect the other squads.

Back in my BOQ tent my thoughts kept turning back to the new houseboy. Then it dawned on me. The "houseboy" was a girl smuggled back from Inchon—and a good-looking one at that. The squad leader, having been warned of my coming, had hidden her in the cab of the halftrack. Contrary to impressions people may have from watching *M*A*S*H,* essentially no females were allowed in the combat zone. The men would probably be fighting over her if she stayed. I called the first sergeant over.

"Sergeant Byrd, I met Sergeant Gonzales's new houseboy today. It occurred to me that Ling may be a girl. Could that be?"

Byrd looked away and said in a low voice, "No sir." It was obvious he was covering up for Gonzales.

"Look, I don't want to see Gonzales facing a court-martial. Tell him she must go immediately."

"Yes sir."

Ling disappeared, and the incident was never mentioned again.

During the three years of war, the Korean civilians had suffered as much as their invaders and defenders, with armies moving up and down the peninsula, destroying their homes and villages. Refugees crowded into the larger cities, living in squalor in makeshift huts. Many of the husbands, fathers, and brothers had been killed or were in the Korean armed services. The families survived any way they could. The many houseboys in our combat units were there to send money back to their families. Prostitution for girls to help feed their families did not carry the stigma that it would have in the United States.

1 March 1953

It's a foggy, warm Sunday morning here in Korea and I feel fresh and in good spirits. I just completed a snappy inspection of the tracks—everything looked sharp and the men seemed to have high morale. Everything seems to be going right. Yesterday was another good day. All the pilots and artillery observers were grounded by cloudy weather, so we horsed around all day. Last night's movie was Happy Times, *a very funny picture. . . .*

Yesterday I was paid $299, but combat pay runs one month behind. . . . I paid Lieutenant Davis the $100 I had borrowed from him (two $50 loans), I sent a money order for $100 to you, and I'm keeping about $130 in cash for PX, houseboys, etc. . . .

With regard to [your question about] income tax, I have until six months after I return from Korea to file income tax statements for the whole time I'm over here. You will have to file a return for money you earned in 1952, but we can file a joint return in January of 1954 for my pay in 1952, and both our incomes in 1953.

Second letter mailed later: *Today I really loafed. . . . Breakfast this morning consisted of broiled steak and eggs, lunch was meat loaf, and tonight was fried chicken. You can see that with such meals I'm not feeling any pangs of hunger.*

2 March 1953

My good deal at the airstrip is ending—I'm being sent up to the 1st Platoon to join Lieutenant Baker again. . . . I'll be working in a field artillery FDC just like Dan [directing quad-50 fire]. Baker and his platoon are situated in the same place as we were [at the 158th Field Artillery Battalion headquarters] before coming to the airstrip . . . tonight I plan to go see Dan. . . . It has been cloudy and snowing, and getting colder throughout the day. . . . I must catch the jeep now to get to Dan's by chow time.

I had been at the airstrip for only fifteen days. During January, A Battery had been the leader in indirect fire, having fired over 241,000 of the 310,000 50-caliber rounds fired. The three other batteries had all quickly mastered the indirect fire technique. In February, the rounds fired by A Battery dropped considerably, and most of them were fired during the first week when my 2nd Platoon was still on the line, participating in the battle for Hill 812. Nevertheless, total rounds fired by the battalion had increased over what it had been in January:

A Battery	107,520
B Battery	188,725
C Battery	78,785
D Battery	<u>95,500</u>
Total rounds	470,530

Lieutenant Whitlock made it clear that I was joining Lieutenant Baker and resuming my duties in the FDC.

3 March 1953

My 2nd Platoon gun crews, which I had been with during my combat time in Korea, would be left behind when I transferred up to the 1st Platoon with Baker. Although we had worked together only a relatively short time, I was reluctant to leave those guys. We had been in the forefront of developing the indirect firing techniques for the quad-50s. We had fought two large battles and fired on enemy targets for many nights during our short association. Even though I was leaving them behind in the safety of the airstrip, I had the feeling that I was deserting the platoon.

Back to the Front

4 March 1953

I'm up here with Baker, and as I said, my job is in the 158th Field Artillery Fire Direction Center. The FDC is a big complicated mass of radios, telephones, drawing boards, instruments, desks, and many maps and charts [and people]. I have a little desk all of my own on which I've set up our AAA indirect firing charts. My job is to be available all day and night to fire our AAA whenever an artillery FO calls for fire on a target. . . . I have one man to help me, and for the past two days we've worked long hours to get it set up to my liking.

Today we fired a good deal and it went pretty smooth to be a new set-up. Dan and I have the same jobs with our respective batteries.

Soon we're going to move up to the BOQ with the cement floor and walled sides that Davis and I left. Now we are living like rats in an old bunker some 100 yards away. I'll be glad when I catch up on things so that I can start slowing down and writing you long letters.

The 158th Field Artillery FDC bunker was large and strongly built, constructed to withstand direct hits from heavy artillery. It was very clean with a concrete floor. Some fifteen officers and enlisted men manned the FDC on a twenty-four hour basis, each with specific assignments. The greatest surprise was electric lights, with their own generator. We were about two miles from the front, but still in perfect range for artillery fire and in range of some mortar. Harassing artillery rounds dropped into the battery area occasionally, throughout the day and more heavily during the nights.

All the quad-50 units with an indirect fire mission in the 45th Division had moved their FDCs in with the field artillery FDCs. This was a big improvement from our former set-up. While field artillery had numerous men in their FDC to direct fire, I was the only AAA FDC officer, along with a telephone man, to direct the fire for the A Battery, 1st Platoon's quad-50s.

The field artillery officer in charge of the FDC showed me to the AAA plotting table, which had the gun positions already surveyed and spotted. The four indirect fire guns were located in permanent positions that did not have to be zeroed in. We were provided two telephones: one, a "hot line" to the guns, and the other, a line to the field artillery switchboard. This switchboard could provide connections with FOs, infantry liaison, Dan, or almost anyone in Korea. Rumors were that more than one enterprising telephone operator had successfully gone through enough switchboard connections to reach his wife or girlfriend in the states (à la *M*A*S*H*).

The first evening, I studied the plotting board and talked to the guns to be sure they were ready. Each of the four guns in indirect firing positions were ordered to fire a burst to be sure everything was working properly. The target was a prominent hill in enemy territory. One of the artillery FOs assured me that each gun was on target. Soon we began to receive firing requests. That first night we fired on targets for several hours, utilizing only one or two of the guns for each target.

In addition to the telephones, a radio had been added for direct contact with infantry. Patrol leaders, in no-man's-land, were allowed to contact me directly by radio. They could call for fire without going through the field artillery FO. This gave them the availability of tremendous firepower—like having four quad-50s tagging along with their patrol.

Some targets were suspected enemy patrols or enemy emplacements, and some were fire requests on known landmarks to help them find their way in the dark. It felt good to be doing a useful job again, and I had a sense of satisfaction about our evening performance. Firing requests usually dropped off after midnight, when most of the patrols had returned to their units. Eventually, in the early morning hours, I left the telephone operator with instructions to call me if necessary and was able to get some sleep in my bunker nearby.

5 March 1953

Lieutenant Whitlock seemed particularly glad to see me. He said that the success of the quad-50 indirect fire in ground combat during the battles for Hill 854 and Hill 812 had attracted a great deal of attention. The battalion staff had evolved new tactics that proved to be a more effective way to deploy the guns. When we were supporting the ROK infantry in Smoke Valley, all eight of my platoon's quad-50s were positioned on or very near the MLR, in direct sight of the enemy. For that reason, we had to camouflage the halftrack or pull it off the ridge to a defilade position (out of sight to the enemy) during daylight hours. Even then, we drew considerable mortar and artillery fire, day and night. During the battle for Hill 812, some of Dan's C Battery quad-50s, in the north end of Smoke Valley, had provided very effective fire from positions in defilade, 2,000 yards or more south of the MLR. These attracted much less enemy fire.

With the new deployment, only three of my platoon's quad-50s would be on the front lines, known as direct fire positions. These would mostly be in sandbag enclosures and would operate as they did in January. However, they were very vulnerable to enemy fire and had a very limited field of fire. These forward guns would be in blocking positions, to be fired primarily to repel direct frontal attacks or in other emergencies. Neither Dan nor I thought that any of the guns should be up on line, but it made the infantrymen feel better to have them there.

The remainder of the platoon's quad-50s would be placed in defilade positions, about 2,000 yards behind our trench lines, for indirect fire. These would be the "workhorses" of the platoon. They were able to fire anytime, day or night, and were less susceptible to enemy fire. A report by Colonel Light listed the advantages of this arrangement:

(1) plunging fire can be delivered in valleys and draws close to the MLR which cannot be reached by direct fire weapons because of their depression limits;

(2) great quantities of fire can be delivered at ranges up to 5000 yards in front of the MLR with comparatively little danger of retaliation since indirect fire positions normally have slight defilade;

(3) By placing indirect fire M-16's under operational control of direct support field artillery battalions, field artillery forward observers and infantry liaison officers can call for quad-50 fire against targets not considered lucrative for field artillery.

The report further stated:

There are no known field manuals nor directives which describe the tactics and techniques for M-16 multiple machine gun employment.

(145th AAA AW Battalion Report, May 1953)

After the 45th Division had moved to the Heartbreak Ridge sector, each quad-50 squad of the 145th AAA AW Battalion, which had been assigned to furnish indirect fire for an infantry regiment, was deployed in defilade positions behind the lines. Since the muzzle blast from indirect fire was not visible, it did not give away gun locations, but tracers appearing from behind a hill did point to their general location. This prompted removal of the tracers from the ammo belts, as we had tried earlier on the MLR. This time it worked. Machine gun rounds would suddenly engulf a target from the sky without warning. The effect was deadly.

Another improvement was that each halftrack had been equipped with a generator to keep the batteries powering the turret charged. Before this addition, it was necessary to keep the halftrack engine running during fire missions.

6 March 1953

Today we moved into the good BOQ. All my time is being taken up by my work in the FDC, as my job is once again to compute data to fire the guns. Now we fire the guns all times of the day and night. Our FDC has developed from a crude board in a frontline hootchie to a very specialized system in the field artillery FDC. It requires long hours and a good deal of mental strain, but it is relatively safe, so I guess it's a good place to be.

I'm reworking all our procedures and incorporating better techniques and improvements wherever I can. I think in another few days I'll have it caught up to my satisfaction. . . .

No-man's-land.

Enemy trenches.

Quad-50 under cover, Tank Hill.

Shelling enemy trenches.

VIEW OF ENEMY LINES FROM UN TRENCHES IN HEARTBREAK RIDGE SECTOR

Preparing to fire on enemy trenches, beyond friendly trenches in foreground.

Squad sergeant on phone hot loop receiving firing data.

Commence firing.

Quad-50 firing on target in continuous bursts.

DAN'S QUAD-50 INDIRECT FIRE ON ENEMY TRENCHES, SPRING 1953

I'm envious of old Mayhall getting out. Over here there's certainly no over-supply of officers, and I can't imagine why they don't ship some of those home-steaders over.

Maybe this war will end soon—we're certainly giving the Commies a harder time than they are giving us.

The next morning I met the platoon's first sergeant. The "top kick" was a big burley Texan who had worked on pipeline construction crews in civilian life. Sergeant Ball had a bully's attitude and was rough with the other enlisted men. Baker thought he was great, but I did not approve of his methods. It was bad enough to be over there without having to put up with a bully for a first sergeant. When one of his subordinates crossed him, he sometimes took the man into the hills and settled the matter with bare fists. He was a throwback from the old army before World War II.

7 March 1953

The weather began to change with a few warmer days, but we had some very heavy, wet snows. We had been told early spring was monsoon season with a lot of rain, but it was still miserably cold at night. On 6 March I was called back to battalion headquarters for a class. Dan and I were now considered the "fathers" of indirect fire for quad-50s. He had built his reputation while I was relaxing at the airstrip and was now considered number one in the FDC operations. Being twins, accustomed to competing with each other, I felt a twinge of jealousy. We demonstrated the FDC techniques to a group of officers, including a "bird" colonel (full colonel). Dan's platoon put on a firing demonstration. While in the class, word filtered down that Joseph Stalin had died in Russia. This caused a lot of speculation that our war would end soon. Everyone lost interest in the class, and soon a bottle appeared and a party ensued. That may seem cruel, but with the misery Stalin had caused the world, he deserved to have his death celebrated.

8 March 1953

It's noon here and I'm writing this from my desk in the FDC. I think I'm getting caught up on my work. We've advanced to the point that I'm beginning to teach enlisted men to work the firing calculations while I supervise. I've got one man [Finch] pretty well trained and I'm looking for another with a high enough IQ and education to pick this up. We're getting more accurate every day, and from all indications we will be used more and more in indirect fire.

I sure would like to be with you this warm, sunny Sunday afternoon. It's been four and a half months since I last saw you and I'm longing to see you again.

Since returning from the airstrip, I had been tied to the FDC every night with fire missions until patrols were all in, usually around two or three hours after midnight. Dan had trained a couple of sergeants to spell him off in the FDC. I complained to Captain Whitlock that we needed more than one FDC operator. He sent me Sergeant Ball to train. I found that Sergeant Ball could barely read, much less calculate the settings for the guns. Whitlock then sent me another sergeant, with about the same results. There had to be some men in the company who were capable. Finally I went to company headquarters and reviewed the personnel files on each of the men in the company. All had taken an aptitude test similar to the civilian IQ test, labeled the "Army General Classification Test." A high score was 100. Both of the sergeants I had tried to teach had scores only in the 30s or 40s. The enlisted man with the highest score in the company was a Corporal Finch, with a score in the 90s. He was the company mechanic who kept the vehicles running. Every job in the army is catalogued by an MOS (Military Occupational Specialty) number, but there was no MOS number for an FDC operator in the quad-50 platoons. When I told Whitlock that I wanted Finch, he hit the ceiling, saying he could not give up the mechanic. I insisted, saying the FDC was more important. He finally conceded, saying he could work the FDC at night and do mechanic work during the day.

That night Finch showed up and quickly mastered the firing technique. Although his hands were grease-stained with black fingernails from the mechanic job, and his fingers were muscular and scarred, making him clumsy with the slide rule, still I knew that I had found the right man. By the end of the evening he was operating the FDC while I observed. By the end of the week I felt comfortable to leave it with him. I had several arguments with Whitlock before Finch was finally relieved of his daylight duties as a mechanic.

9 March 1953

Thereafter, Finch and I took turns in the FDC and had phone operators to assist. If a lot of action developed we both joined in. On off nights I could take a leisurely dinner and bar drinks with the other officers, followed by the nightly movie. Also, I was able to visit the squads in action at night to watch their performance. As time passed Finch took on more and more of the FDC work. I looked for someone to help him but had a hard time finding another man of his caliber.

10 March 1953

My job in the FDC is desk work but it sure keeps me busy. It's the middle of the afternoon and there's plenty of work yet to be done, but I'm going to stop the war and write to you. . . .

Today here is foggy and warm with the gray ceiling resting on the peaks of these steep bare mountains. . . .

Guess I'd better close. One of my guns is trained on a hole where we chased two Chinks with machine gun burst this morning. When they stick their heads out, the artillery observer telephones me and I telephone the tracks to fire. In about thirty seconds, the Chinks suddenly get a rain of machine gun bullets around their hole—we're giving them a hard time. By means of our FDC, the tracks are three miles away firing on the hole—the Chinks can't tell where the rounds are coming from.

11 March 1953

Today has been highlighted by the weather. There was a heavy layer of snow covering everything when I awoke this morning, and it has snowed most of the day. It has been a quiet day for us with nothing much happening.

I have a new man [Jones] training to work in the FDC, and I spent most of the day teaching him our procedures. If he works out, I will start a full twenty-four-hour shift in the FDC and start training a third man to assist the two already adapted to it. . . .

The FDC has a radio that we can tune in to soft music when no missions are under way. It makes me think of you.

12 March 1953

The snow continued all night and on up until noon today. We are almost snowbound. It's early afternoon, and the sun is out, making the outdoors dazzlingly bright.

I couldn't find any place to buy your birthday present, so I can only wish you a Happy Birthday and will make it up next year. . . .

Things are pretty slow around the FDC. . . . Heavy snow has hidden the enemy from us for a day and a half now. The snow is so deep that the rounds bury themselves in it and can't be seen by the observer. . . .

Today I received your letter about plans to make Texas A&M coed. I'm very much against it, of course, as is every other Aggie I know.

The Air Strike

13 March 1953

At lunch the air liaison officer, Lieutenant Harwood, said he would be directing an air strike against the enemy on Heartbreak Ridge that afternoon and invited me and Baker to go along with him to see the action. We quickly accepted. After eating, our driver fell in behind Lieutenant Harwood's jeep, which also carried his radio operator and driver, and followed them to the front lines. He parked on top of a ridge just behind the trench line, which had a good view of the enemy trenches and hills. Some brightly colored panels had been put out along the friendly trenches, which could be spotted from the air but not by the enemy.

About forty-five minutes later, we heard the sound of approaching jets. Harwood began to talk to the pilots on the radio, directing them into position for the bombing. The squadron of jets came into view at a high altitude. As we watched, the lead plane peeled off and began a steep dive. It looked at first as if he was diving at us, but as he screamed downward it became obvious that the target was the hill behind the enemy trenches. A single enemy machine gun began firing at the diving plane—ack-ack-ack, accompanied by fire from some small arms. It looked as though he might dive the jet right into the ground, but at the last minute he pulled out of the dive, leaving behind a 500-pound bomb hurtling toward the target. There was a deafening explosion, and a large cloud of black smoke rose from the back side of the hill. A second jet followed the first. Ignoring the ack-ack-ack of the single machine gun, it dived and released a second bomb. Another explosion and black smoke shot upwards. One after another in similar fashion, the squadron's planes bombed the target.

About the seventh plane to dive pulled up prematurely. His bomb came sailing toward friendly lines and exploded about 500 yards west of us. We speculated that he had been hit by the lone machine gun, but he may have just panicked and pulled up too soon. Whatever the reason, the bombing attack was called off, and the planes headed back to the base. We later learned that the stray bomb had hit in a group of ROKs watching the bombing, killing five and wounding several more. I decided then that when huge amounts of explosives are being dropped from the sky, it may not be such a good idea to stand around and watch.

14 March 1953

I missed writing you yesterday because the colonel [in the FDC] doesn't like to catch anyone writing letters. Also we were very busy. I spend from twelve to fourteen hours a day here in the FDC, as I don't feel it's safe yet to leave it with the enlisted men (EM). All our firing is over the heads of friendly troops. A slight miscalculation and we'd be shooting up our infantry. The way I'm working it now is two twelve-hour shifts for the EM. One comes from noon to midnight, and the other from midnight to noon. I overlap a portion of both their shifts from breakfast until about nine o'clock at night. I will be here when most of the firing is conducted. We're getting better all the time, and I believe we are really developing something new for the army.

It's snowing again today, which cuts down on our firing. The weather is warm, just right for snow.

15 March 1953

The weather has been warm and fair, which resulted in us being busy. It's about 7:00 PM and I'm still busy. I'm going to take time to write you anyway. . . .

I am very proud of you for being photographed as the most beautiful "law woman" in Texas, for the Oak Cliff Tribune. *. . . [Robbie worked in the constable's office in Oak Cliff, a part of Dallas.]*

P.S. In answer to your question, my lips have healed nicely with no scars.

16 March 1953

It's now late Monday night and I can hardly remember where the day went. Here in the FDC things are now quiet. We're sitting around, waiting to see if some of the infantry patrols are going to make enemy contact. We have our tracks set on points just ahead of the area where there is most likely to be a fight and stay ready to spray the points to prevent any reinforcements or retreat of the enemy when the fight starts. This is just routine, but I thought you might be interested in how we're operating.

The radio in here is filling the bunker with soft, dreamy music, a very favorable atmosphere for thinking of you. The artillery and "ack-ack" alike are sitting around writing letters (the S-3 is not here). In spite of all the activity and rush of the day, thoughts and dreams of you always linger in my mind.

I got a letter today from Al Besteiro [an Aggie] who is stationed on Kŏje-Do Island [the Korean prison camp near Pusan]. He seems to be living a life of ease. Dan is coming tomorrow with the chaplain who lives in his BOQ.

20 March 1953

Today has been damp and muddy, but all in all it's been a pretty good day. The FDC is operating so smoothly that I'm getting real satisfaction from it. The quad-50s are becoming a really effective weapon in indirect fire.

Today we tried several new projects to improve their effectiveness, and the results were good. A major, a colonel, and several captains came in to look over our set-up today. All were pleased. The procedures were generally over their heads, but our results speak for themselves.

21 March 1953

With the snow beginning to melt, the squads began to explore and clean up around their gun positions. One of the squad leaders reported that they had found a skeleton in a cave and they thought it was a US Marine. A piece of tent canvas by its side was wrapped about a Thompson submachine gun, a weapon that was issued to marines earlier in the war. The Thompson was a machine gun similar to those used by gangsters in the old 1920s movies, identified by the round circular shell canister. Graves Registration was notified of the skeleton, but the squad kept the machine gun and cleaned it up. It fired 45-caliber shells, the same as our side arms. Soon they were practice-firing it. I fired it a couple of times but found it climbed skyward with each round fired. Obviously the handle in front was there to hold it down by main force. It was not a very dependable weapon.

22 March 1953

Yesterday our battery commander [Whitlock] got back from R&R so I went to see him last night. He was thinking about moving Baker and me back to the airstrip and moving the other platoon up.

If Whitlock moved Lieutenant Davis's platoon up, it would probably be necessary to leave the FDC men, including me, at the present location. There was no one in Hamp's platoon familiar enough with the indirect firing technique to operate the FDC. Whitlock apparently realized this and abandoned the idea.

23 March 1953

Today has been a typical day working in the FDC. We chase Chinks every time one shows himself. . . . Dan called to say he would try to come over tomorrow, so we can loaf and talk oil. . . . The monotony of the FDC gets on your nerves.

. . .

    The enlisted men I have working with me were glad to hear that I would be with them another month. It's gratifying to know they like to work with me even though I keep them pretty busy. Through the grapevine, I hear that Dan and I are considered the two smartest officers in the battalion. . . . I'm not bragging, you understand, but telling you (my wife) should be permissible.

    Dan and I were both put in for first lieutenant several weeks ago. . . . I guess we'll make it. [Although we were not the best examples of shavetail officers.]

24 March 1953

The colonel [Colonel Light] came out to inspect the tracks tonight, then went up to an observation post with the artillery FO to fire some of the tracks at targets he selected.

Colonel Light had come a long way since arriving at the battalion in late January. For the first few weeks, he appeared completely unaware of the niche his quad-50s held in providing ground support for the infantry. And he had been oblivious of the role the quad-50 had played in the battles for Hill 854 and Hill 812, which were initially left out of his monthly reports. He learned the details of the action later. Once he realized the role the quad-50s were playing, however, he became one of their most enthusiastic supporters in indirect fire.

With the quad-50 FDCs operating in the same bunker as the field artillery FDC, there was a glaring contrast in the instruments available for calculating firing data between the field artillery and the ack-ack. The field artillery had Graphic Firing Tables (GFT) and Graphic Site Tables (GST), which reduced reams of tabular data to a few parallel rows of numbers on slide rules. Using these, the FDC personnel could produce data to align the guns on a target within seconds. The quad-50 operators, however, had to make their calculations from pages of tables in manuals in order to furnish the data necessary to calculate the gun settings. This resulted in several minutes' delay before firing data could be relayed to the guns.

Colonel Light decided that we should develop a GFT and a GST for the quad-50 by converting the pages of tables to slide rules. Since we operated with only a single FDC operator, it would be desirable to have all the data combined on a single slide rule. The colonel directed his adjutant, Capt. Harris A. McCormack, to locate a team to develop such a device.

25 March 1953

At noon I'm going into the battery for lunch, then on to battalion for a class.

At the battalion class that afternoon, the possibility of developing a GFT for the quad-50 FDC was brought up. It was decided that a field artillery officer who was proficient in the operation of the field artillery's GFT and GST should direct the project. A young first lieutenant who had been operating one of the quad-50 FDCs in the battalion was assigned the job of working with the artillery officer.

26 March 1953

Today I walked all morning making a round of our tracks. After lunch I took a shower—my first in three weeks [we'd been busy]. It's been a pretty good day with very little of my time being required in the FDC. The only complaint I have is that no mail came in tonight.

27 March 1953

Some nights we were shelled for hours with little letup. In the FDC bunker, which was strongly built, we felt safe. In our hootchies we felt less secure, not knowing if they would withstand a direct hit on the roof. When bombardments began at night, I would spread my open flak jacket over my private parts and chest, with my steel helmet over my face. Even with the explosions going off outside, I managed to get some sleep.

28 March 1953

Construction had been started on a new squad bunker down the valley from us. When the sides were completed but before the roof was finished, the squad began sleeping in it. One night an 82 mm mortar fell inside the enclosure, killing or badly wounding all ten men. Their luck had run out. But there was also a nagging doubt that the round was too well placed to be just luck. Was there an infiltrator hiding in the hills secretly directing fire?

29 March 1953

Today was quite eventful. We were assigned a new officer [in the platoon] by the name of Bill Reimus, who will be my understudy in the FDC. He seems to be a good guy, and I believe he will be able to pick up the FDC operation OK.

Also, we made an advance in delivering "ack-ack" fire. There is a ridge near Heartbreak from which the enemy gives my regimental infantry trouble every night. The ridge is shielded from the fire from my guns by a higher friendly hill, and I've racked my brain for a way to give our troops support on that ridge. Today I got an idea and kicked myself for not thinking of it sooner. Dan's platoon supports the infantry regiment on my right. It occurred to me that he may be able to reach the enemy ridge with one of his guns, even though it is out of his regimental sector. I went over to see him. We compared our capabilities and found that he could reach it not with just one but with no fewer than four of his tracks. We got the ball rolling by notifying the S-3 of the field artillery battalion. Soon he sent communication men to add frequencies to our radios so we could talk directly between platoons. We now have the firepower of both platoons coordinated to a well-running machine that is going to give the Chinks a mighty hard time. The Chinks should know better than to trifle with us, especially when the Hughes brothers get their heads together.

In the Heartbreak Ridge sector we were opposed by Chinese instead of North Koreans. Their aggressiveness was governed primarily by the progress of the Panmunjom Peace Talks, which had been in recess since the impasse of 8 October 1952. On 28 March 1953, the Communist leaders signaled that they were ready to resume the talks and favored the exchange of sick and wounded prisoners of war. They had learned that the United States had shipped a secret weapon to the FECOM: a 280 mm (eleven-inch) cannon capable of firing a nuclear warhead as well as conventional artillery shells. If the cannon were used in frontline combat, the catacomb of caves that protected the Communist troops could become mass graves. This may have influenced the Communists' decision to resume the talks (Fehrenbach 1963, 442).

During the third Korean winter campaign, the Communists had built up their forces to over a million by the end of January and had stockpiled ammunition and rations at the front. Three Chinese armies and one Korean corps had been replaced by fresh troops that were fully equipped and trained for combat (Hermes 1966, 389).

Rather than there being a slowdown in artillery action on the front lines as the Panmunjom talks resumed, there was an increase. "In the spring of 1953 the Communists decided to use the battlefield to apply pressure upon the [Panmunjom] negotiations and to prepare some basis for their claim of military victory" (Hermes 1966, 508). If the talks were going in their favor, action was light. If the talks reached an impasse, the Communists became very aggressive. Their principal means of showing displeasure was by increased mortar and artillery fire. Attacks were made whenever the talks seemed to reach an insurmountable obstacle.

Second Lieutenant Reimus

30 March 1953

On 27 March 1953, Dan and I were promoted to first lieutenants. Both of us were in line to be the next commanders of our platoons when the present platoon leaders rotated. The quad-50s had become so popular that we were given priority for replacement personnel. Lt. William J. Reimus had been assigned to my platoon on 28 March. Reimus was a college graduate from Wisconsin, fresh out of OCS, very intelligent, and just what we needed for the FDC. He moved into the BOQ with Baker and me to be my subordinate when Baker left. His first day was spent visiting the guns.

The four halftracks in permanent firing position near our BOQ were out of sight from the enemy and could fire during the daytime with little risk of retaliation. We fired at a few targets of our choosing to let Reimus see how the gun crews operated. These indirect firing methods were still not being taught at Fort Bliss, so it was up to us to pass on what we had learned.

We waited until after dark to take Reimus to the three forward quad-50s in direct fire, as these positions were under enemy observation. The direct fire quad-50 halftracks were dug in on high ground just behind the infantry trenches. Each had overhead protection from a canopy of sandbag-covered logs. The four barrels of each turret pointed menacingly at the enemy's trench line through an opening in the rear of the embattlement. These quad-50s were seldom fired because of their exposed position but could give direct fire in case of a major attack. We visited each of our direct fire guns and talked to the crews. There was very little firing going on up and down the line at the time.

After leaving our direct fire quad-50 positions, we climbed down into the infantry trenches. The infantry platoon leader, a first lieutenant, led us down the trench to his command post bunker. He was very complimentary of the support that he was getting from the ack-ack and offered us coffee. Afterward he led us further down the trenches to an area that was dimly illuminated by diffused light from a powerful overhead beam. This unmoving beam originated from a giant searchlight on a hill behind the trench line, which produced a cylinder of light that fell brightly on the enemy trenches 1,500 yards across the valley. It was an eerie but sobering sight.

Baker, Reimus, and I each had our carbine slung on our backs with "banana" clips of ammo but no round in the chamber, to prevent accidental firing. The ground in front of the trench dropped off sharply into darkness. Suddenly two Korean soldiers came up the hill into the light, their rifles held at the ready positon. Reimus panicked, jerked up his carbine, put a round in its chamber, and pointed it at the advancing Koreans. We yelled for him to stop and pushed the barrel of his rifle skyward. He did not fire. We had forgotten to explain to him about the KATUSAs, Korean soldiers attached to American units. These KATUSAs were returning from patrol and never realized how close they had come to getting shot. The infantry platoon leader guiding us was amused by the whole episode.

The next day I introduced Reimus to the operations of the FDC. He quickly grasped the indirect fire procedures. Thanks to Reimus, Finch, and Jones, I would be largely free of FDC duties. I admit that I felt somewhat reluctant to give up what was partly my creation, but after just a few days Reimus had actually improved the system, especially the recordkeeping. A report of each fire mission was carefully recorded, giving the location, time, number of rounds fired, and the results. This became standard procedure for all indirect fire missions within the battalion.

31 March 1953

I got paid $129 today. I'm having a money order made out to you for $150, which, [with the money I have] will leave me about $70 until next payday.

Today the radio said the Chinks were about to accept the UN Prisoner Repatriation Proposal. To make us even more hopeful, several Chinese came over to our lines and gave themselves up to my regimental sector. They said more are waiting to do the same. I would like to see this thing come to an end.

We ack-ack officers have a lot of fun kidding the artillery officers. We say the artillery has been shooting at the Chinks for three years with no effect, and we come in and start firing indirect fire and make them surrender in three months.

Also, we tell them that we are going to start using miniature smoke rounds in our quad-50s, like the big smoke shells the artillery uses. We'll spray the area with these small smoke shells and the enemy will think they're cigarette butts. When they come out of their holes to police them up, we'll open up on them. We keep the day lively trying to outwit the field artillery officers.

The Short Round

1 April 1953

The American press was making a big issue of ammunition shortages in Korea. It was true that certain calibers of artillery and mortar ammunition were limited. The intensity of the barrages exceeded anything in either World War I or World War II, and already by the beginning of 1953, more explosive shells (artillery, mortar, tank, etc.) had been fired in Korea than all those fired in either of the two world wars (Fehrenbach 1963, 439). The enemy had as many field guns as did the UN but they did not put out the volume of fire, possibly due to air interdiction of their supply lines.

The use in our battalion of quad-50s in ground support steadily increased after their first use in January 1953. Rounds fired in the month of February totaled 470,530—up 52 percent from the number fired in January. And the total for March was 726,968—up 55 percent from the total rounds fired in February. These large increases became a logistics problem. It took a fleet of trucks to deliver these large volumes of 50-caliber machine gun ammunition (belts of rounds in canisters) and to carry away the tons of spent brass (over fifty tons in March alone). Also, barrel replacement became a serious problem, requiring several hundred new barrels per month for the battalion.

In typical army fashion, the cost of each 50-caliber round and the cost of each new barrel were posted at squad CPs, with instructions to not waste any rounds. When a patrol or frontline observer called for fire, did they expect us to ask, "Is this fire necessary?" We laughed at the idea, but Lieutenant Baker thought he would do his part. He ordered that barrels would be fired to 90 percent of wear before being discarded rather than 70 percent, as was the current practice. I argued with him that at 90 percent there was not a great enough safety factor, especially since we were still using the homemade gauges to check the wear. But Baker wouldn't budge on the issue.

2 April 1953

I finally made first lieutenant. Already, I've given away $11 worth of cigars. . . . This will mean an additional $45.76 per month—we're getting rich.

Lieutenant Baker is going on R&R tomorrow to Japan. I'm turning over the FDC to the new officer, Reimus, and I will take over as platoon leader for the next ten days. I don't particularly want the job, but it will be a change. . . .

Incidentally, Dan made first lieutenant on the same orders that I did, so we don't outrank each other. . . . I've been thinking about coming home. . . .

I wouldn't stay away from you for a minute longer than I have to, even if they made me a general.

3 April 1953

I received your birthday party pictures and the certificate making me a constable in Oak Cliff. I am proud to be a constable—you must have a lot of influence. . . .

Baker left on R&R, and problems have been arising all over the place. I'm writing this in the middle of the afternoon because I'm supposed to go in tonight to see the colonel. . . . I'll sure be glad when Baker returns.

4 April 1953

Today is Easter Sunday but it was just another workday over here, and harder than usual. I'm writing this in my sleeping bag being too tired to sit up [I went to sleep at this point].

By Easter Sunday, 4 April, the days were becoming much warmer, although the nights were still below freezing. Occasional days were windy and cold, but spring was definitely in the air. We began to wear wool clothes and leather boots in lieu of the padded coats and Mickey Mouse boots. The snow melted, trees put out new leaves, and flowers bloomed. After spending most of our time indoors during the cold weather, we began to venture into the hills and countryside.

Dan decided to hike up a trail that had become accessible when the snow melted. As he walked along, picking his way, he was about to step down when he saw three short prongs sticking out of the ground—the trip fuse of a land mine. Realizing he was in an old unmarked minefield, he slowly backed away, trying to step exactly where he had stepped going in. Back at his hootchie, he called the engineers to mark off the area and label it a minefield. He then called to warn me of the danger. Land mines are the most dreaded scourge in warfare. Although seldom fatal, they result in the loss of legs, reproductive organs, arms, and eyes; they leave one crippled for life.

5 April 1953

I'll finish the letter that I started last night. . . . Everyone over here is encouraged by the resumption of peace talks, although the war hasn't let up any.

Tonight I'm going over to see Dan. He and I are going to give a class to the rest of the battalion officers on the operation of the Fire Direction Center (FDC in case you forgot). . . . This will take place on Wednesday and Thursday nights, so we'll be working on that. Also, I'll probably stay over and see a movie. . . .

Last night Dan and I massed fire from all our tracks on one point. We had fourteen quad-50 tracks all hitting the same point at the same time, using incendiary ammunition. It made quite a show. . . .

Rumors of a truce are getting thick around here. One captain is willing to bet $50 that the war will end this month. I'm afraid to believe any of them, myself.

The Generals' Shoot

The higher echelons of command in the 45th Division were very much pleased with the growing use of the quad-50s to support the infantry. However, some were not convinced that weapons located a mile or more behind the trenches were as effective as those on the line with the infantry in direct firing positions.

One argued, "If they're up there on the line with the infantry, they can mow down the Chinks, like in World War I. Let them come charging, blowing their bugles and yelling. The searchlights let the gunners see the bastards and blow them to hell."

Another officer countered, "That sounds good, but it doesn't work that way. Guns too close to the front are pretty much limited to targets right out front and cannot depress to fire on enemy climbing up to their position. They're going to get a hell of a lot of return fire. The gun crew is likely to take cover if it gets too heavy. Guns in defilade around 2,000 yards back can lob rounds down on targets over a much wider range, as much as 5,000 yards in front of our trench lines. They can fire for long periods undetected with only minimal return fire. They have the advantage of surprise when 50-caliber rounds drop down out of nowhere, on enemy troops way behind their lines."

Brig. Gen. P. D. Ginder, commander of the 45th Division, decided to see for himself. He invited Lt. Gen. I. D. White, the X Corps commander, to join him. The general's aid notified Lieutenant Colonel Light that he wanted a demonstration of indirect fire by quad-50 units. Colonel Light called my battery commander, Whitlock, and Dan's battery commander, McDonough, to arrange a demonstration shoot. Not surprisingly, Dan and I were assigned the task.

Heartbreak Ridge is the southern, UN-held portion of a much longer ridge tending north-south. It drops off sharply to the east and west into river valleys. The ridge rises about 1,400 feet above the Mungdung-ni valley floor, with several high points along the north-south axis. The opposing trench lines, which cross the ridge, are separated by a cut that is about 400 feet lower than the ridge on either side. Communists held the portion north of the depression, and UN troops held the two miles of ridgeline to the south, known as Heartbreak Ridge. The high peak on our side, from where the generals would observe, was Hill 931, about one mile south of our trench line. On the enemy side, the ridgeline rose steadily for about two miles. There was a trail along the crest that the enemy used only at night. We picked a portion of this trail that was in full view of Hill 931 for our target.

Each of our platoons had four halftracks, or eight guns, that were located to deliver indirect fire. We did not believe this was enough, so we included guns from each platoon that were in direct fire positions but far enough back to double as indirect fire weapons, giving us a total of fourteen M-16s. We assigned each gun a portion of the ridge along the trail.

To have a more dramatic effect, we decided to fire a "TOT" (time on target), where the first round from all the guns would hit the ground at the same time. For example, it only takes seven seconds for a round to travel 3,000 yards, but it takes twenty-three seconds to travel 6,000 yards (see fig. 1, p. 154). By calculating a travel time from each gun separately, we could call on them to fire in an order that would accomplish the TOT. We loaded all four machine guns on each turret with a full magazine of ammunition (two hundred rounds each) and prepared to fire them simultaneously—normally we only fired two and kept two in reserve. Darkness had fallen by the time we were ready. Our crews were on the guns waiting on the order to fire. Besides impressing the general, we felt sure we would catch some Chinks in the open, along the trail.

About an hour later, one of the officers from battalion headquarters contacted us by radio, saying that the generals were in position on Hill 931. We reported that we were ready. A moment later the voice commanded, "Commence firing!" The gun farthest from the target required twenty-two seconds' travel time. Using the second hand on his watch, Dan began to read the seconds over the hot loop, 22–21–20–19–18, etc. Each gunner had been told at which second he should begin firing. As each gun opened up, it continued to fire with long bursts until the entire magazine was empty, which took several minutes. Dan and I were in the FDCs and could not witness the target area, but later reports from men with the generals said it was the most spectacular display they had ever witnessed. Wave after wave

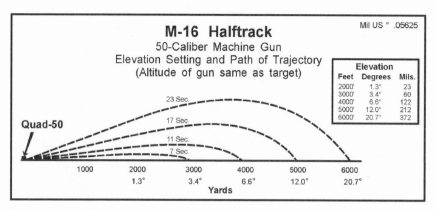

FIGURE I DIAGRAM OF QUAD-50 FIRE

of sparkling explosions raked several hundred yards of the ridgeline. The whole ridge appeared to be on fire.

After the last guns went silent, we were caught with our pants down when the general ordered, "Repeat!" Too late, we realized that we should have fired only half of our magazines and be prepared to fire again. Instead, we had to completely reload all the guns and change barrels in some cases. To make it worse, an infantry officer called Dan to say one of his guns had fired into the hillside behind his trenches.

Dan told him, "We're firing for General Ginder and he wants us to fire again. We're reloading and changing some of the barrels now. This should fix the problem, but just in case, keep your heads down."

The infantryman reluctantly said, "Okay."

It took about ten minutes to be ready to fire again. The second round was as spectacular as the first, but the long pause between the firings had cast a shadow on our otherwise glorious performance. If we had followed normal procedure, we would have been all right.

6 April 1953

After four months in combat, both officers and enlisted men were awarded five days (or more) of "rest and relaxation" in Japan. Periodically, each squad was allocated two cases of beer. During the time Baker was away on R&R, the beer ration came in. Sergeant Ball drove by each squad, throwing out two cases of beer as he passed.

That night I was in the FDC, where we were firing missions, when a call came in from an infantry unit forward of us saying that we had fired rounds

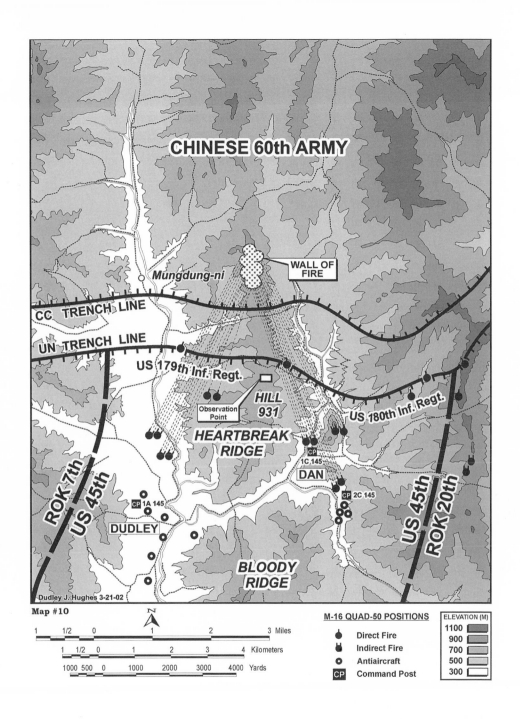

CHINESE 60th ARMY

Mungdung-ni

WALL OF
FIRE

CC TRENCH LINE

UN TRENCH LINE

US 179th Inf. Regt.

Observation
Point

HILL
931

US 180th Inf. Regt.

HEARTBREAK
RIDGE

CP
1C 145

DAN

CP 2C 145

ROK 7th

US 45th

CP 1A 145

DUDLEY

BLOODY
RIDGE

US 45th

ROK 20th

Dudley J. Hughes 3-21-02

Map #10

N

| 1 | 1/2 | 0 | 1 | 2 | 3 Miles |

| 1 | 1/2 | 0 | 1 | 2 | 3 | 4 Kilometers |

| 1000 500 | 0 | 1000 | 2000 | 3000 | 4000 Yards |

M-16 QUAD-50 POSITIONS

- Direct Fire
- Indirect Fire
- Antiaircraft
- CP Command Post

ELEVATION (M)
1100
900
700
500
300

MAP 10 THE GENERALS' SHOOT, 4 APRIL 1953

into their area and had hit one of their men. From their location I could tell the fire must have come from gun #4.

"All guns, cease fire. Gun #4, the infantry in the direction of your fire reports that 50-caliber rounds dropped into their area and hit a man. Have you checked your barrels?"

"Yes Sir, we have a barrel that burned out before we caught it." More details came from the infantry. The rounds had fallen behind the lines and through a jeep's roof, hitting a private driver in the fleshly part of his thigh. I called Finch to come and take Reimus's place in the FDC and notified Whitlock of the incident. Waking my driver, we took off for gun #4. The squad leader had the barrel lying on a table. The makeshift gauge showed the inside of the barrel was 100 percent worn. The squad leader smelled strongly of beer, as did several of the squad. I had the driver take what beer was left and put it in my jeep.

We drove back to the FDC and found Whitlock there. He said the commanding officer of the 45th Division Field Artillery battalions had learned of the incident and wanted us to report to him the next day. I asked Finch to notify each squad that we were reverting to our old method of pulling barrels when they were 70 percent worn. Also, we had the squad leader of gun #4 bring the burned-out barrel, plus a new barrel and the barrel gauge. We would need those for the meeting with the colonel the next day.

7 April 1953

The next morning I canceled all future beer rations to guns on the firing line. Later my driver took me to the field hospital, a group of tents back near the airstrip, where the wounded man was lying in bed reading a book. Introducing myself, I apologized for the wound we had inflicted upon him.

"Are you in any pain?" I asked.

"No, sir, it's just in the muscle of my leg. It doesn't hurt at all. In fact, this is a million-dollar wound—I'll get to rotate home. I'm kind of glad it happened."

I couldn't share his enthusiasm as I was about to catch hell over it.

Late that afternoon, Lieutenant Whitlock and I met with the colonel, the commanding officer of the division's field artillery battalions. He was a tough, old-time bird colonel who kept us standing at attention while he chewed us out for several minutes. Eventually he calmed down enough to hear our explanation of the incident. Whitlock demonstrated the difference between the worn and new barrels with the makeshift gauge. The gauge consisted of a 50-caliber projectile fastened to a welding rod with calibrated marks filed along the rod. The reading was not always precise, as the amount of pressure applied to the rod affected its reading, leaving it to the discretion of the gun handler to determine the pressure to use. Whitlock suggested that if we had been able to obtain the standard gauge called for in the Table of Organization and Equipment (TO&E), we might have avoided the accident.

The Colonel pursued a different course. He asked me, "How much clearance do you allow for overhead fire?"

"Ten yards, sir."

"What does the quad-50 manual call for?"

"Twenty yards, sir. But that is with uncontrolled overhead fire. We are using indirect fire methods similar to the field artillery. It's safe to use a smaller clearance."

"If the manual calls for 20 yards, then I want you to go to 20 yards."

I argued, "But sir, if the barrel burned out, the rounds would still have dropped short regardless of the clearance. Our no-fire zone will move out and many of our targets will be off-limits."

"Those are my orders, Lieutenant. You're dismissed."

We saluted and left.

I was still smarting from the scolding when Whitlock dropped me off at my FDC. He cautioned me to follow the colonel's orders. On my firing chart, I recalculated the no-fire zone, using the higher limits. Much of no-man's-land was now off-limits. We would be greatly hamstrung in our efforts to help the infantry patrols. Only rarely did we have to depress fire to minimum clearance.

Firing was slack during the first part of the evening. Around midnight I had radio contact from a twelve-man patrol moving about between the friendly trenches and the enemy trenches. A lieutenant in charge, in a low voice said, "We are lost out here and would like for you to fire a burst on Hill 756 so we can locate ourselves."

I looked at the firing chart. Hill 756 was now in the no-fire zone.

"I'm sorry, Lieutenant, but Hill 756 is in the no fire zone."

"What do you mean? You have fired on it for us several times in the past."

"I know, but beginning today, the Field Artillery Division commanding officer put it off limits."

"Listen, we're in trouble out here. We don't know the way back to our lines. We might stumble into a minefield. This is serious, some of us could die. Just give us one little burst."

I knew he was right. I also knew that I could probably get away with it. I was torn between firing the burst or obeying orders. My sense of military discipline finally won out.

"I'm sorry, but I can't disobey a direct order."

My radio went dead. I never learned if they found their way back with no casualties. I've kicked myself many times for not firing the burst. If I had a chance to do it over again, I would fire on Hill 756 until I ran out of ammunition. This still haunts me fifty years later.

The next morning I passed the story on to Whitlock. He apparently talked to the colonel again, because the order was rescinded and we were allowed to go back to our previous no-fire line of only ten yards' overhead clearance. It was too late to help those poor bastards who were wandering around in no-man's-land the night before.

8 April 1953

I've been "snowed under" the past few days, so once again I'm writing this letter from my sleeping bag before I go to sleep. . . . It's after midnight and I have to get up early in the morning.

9 April 1953

I want to apologize for not writing the past few days, but I've had many problems and much work. I'm sick of this army—it's a thankless job with a big collection of eight-balls running it.

Following the shooting incident, a directive came from battalion regarding 50-caliber fire:

Barrels
a) Change barrels after firing 200 rounds, cool, and gauge before firing again.
b) Barrels of approximately equal wear are grouped and used together.
c) Barrels must be gauged regularly and those showing wear of 13 gradations (~70%) or more will be salvaged.
d) Each M-16 will maintain at least 12 spare barrels.

(145th AAA AW Battalion Reports, May 1953)

10 April 1953

I have been so busy that I sort of lost track of time. Baker sure went on R&R at a bad time. . . . It's 1:30 and I've got to get up at 5:00. I think that starting tomorrow I'll have more time off.

Dan and I gave a class to the battalion officers yesterday and again today. It went pretty well—got lots of compliments.

11 April 1953

When Baker returns, I think I may get to change jobs. Lieutenant Reimus is about trained to run the FDC. The tension from working in the FDC has been getting on my nerves. I believe I may crack up if I have to stay there much longer. . . .

The battery commander says he might consider bringing me into battery headquarters to straighten out the records, which the executive officer has in pretty much of a mess.

12 April 1953

I'm expecting Lieutenant Baker back tonight or tomorrow and I sure will be glad to see him. . . . We're doing a lot of firing now, but I've shoved off the FDC on Lieutenant Reimus.

Lieutenant Baker returned from R&R, and I was glad to turn the reins of command back over to him. His decision to allow barrels to be fired to 90 percent wear had heaped days of misery on me, but he was oblivious to the seriousness of the ordeal. His stay in Japan had achieved "relaxation."

One of the first things a serviceman did when he arrived in Japan was to call home. The large number of telephone calls being made to the States greatly overloaded the system. Therefore, it was necessary to place a call and wait as much as several days for it to go through. When it eventually went through, the operator would ring you at the number you had provided. Baker told the story of one man in his group who was in bed with a cute Japanese girl when the call to his wife came through. His wife had not talked with him for eight months, and at the sound of his voice she burst out crying. The husband was trying to console her so they could talk. The little Japanese girl began to tickle him in the ribs. He couldn't help but laugh. She tickled harder. He couldn't stop laughing, while the wife couldn't stop crying. Not everyone thought it was funny, but Baker kept everyone entertained with stories all evening.

13 April 1953

There's been a revision of policy on the departure of reserve officers . . . , allowing rotation in nineteen to twenty-two and a half months [of active duty]. . . . It's encouraging to know that I am eligible to leave anytime after the 26th of this month. . . . I've already started to let my hair grow out. . . . Of course, the whole thing is pretty indefinite.

As the days got longer, great changes came over the Korean countryside. One that caught us all by surprise was the appearance of thousands of green frogs with bright red spots. The streams were choked with them, as was the spring where we got our water. Even though the water was always treated with chlorine, we could not use the springwater because of the slime and frog eggs. Water had to be hauled in from distant places in tank trucks. The road became slick in places where hundreds of frogs trying to cross were squashed by passing vehicles.

The light colonel commanding the field artillery battalion to which we were attached ordered all off-duty personnel to accompany him on a hike into the hills each morning to get in shape. I didn't think the order would apply to our unit since we were not part of the field artillery, but the next morning Baker and I were unceremoniously rousted out of our sleeping bags soon after daylight.

"The colonel is waiting for you both outside."

"What does he want?"

"You were supposed to be in the group going on the hike."

Hurriedly dressing, we went outside and ran to catch the tail end of the hikers going up the hill. The colonel hiked at a fast pace. We were quickly winded. Remembering Dan's warning about land mines I stayed on the pathway well traveled by those ahead. The hike lasted about an hour and had us sweating, even in cool weather. These hikes became routine, and we actually did get in shape. The colonel was right.

14 April 1953

I was mildly surprised that you were interested in our war problems over here [a reference to Robbie's last letter]. I could have relayed many stories to you of our experiences, but I thought it best to save them until I got home.

Dan and I have been given a lot of credit for making the quad-50s an effective weapon for indirect firing. When we first got here, they were just beginning to experiment with it. Now it is a quick, accurate, and very devastating type of firepower. . . .

I've turned the FDC over to Reimus. Baker and I are taking care of the platoon together. We're having it pretty easy, as you can guess.

There are lots of new replacements coming in, and it won't be long before the entire battery will have changed hands.

We're waiting on the division to decide what policy they will use to rotate the officers who have completed nineteen months or more [of active duty. The consensus of the ranking officers was that the number of points required for rotation would soon be reduced.]

15 April 1953

Baker and I will inspect the tracks this morning and "survey in" a couple this afternoon [for indirect fire]. Last night Dan came over with a new lieutenant [Frank Malone from Texas], and we played cards. The main topic of conversation was "early release." Everyone is waiting to hear the division's policy.

There is a camera crew today taking shots of the operation of our quad-50 FDC to make a training film to use back in the States.

Colonel Light's effort to develop a GFT for the quad-50 machine guns was close to being accomplished. The field artillery FDC officers contributed a great deal. They began by taking a field artillery GFT and sandpapering all the numbers off the face of it. Then data taken from the quad-50 field manuals was transposed by hand to rows of numbers on the slide rule base. Figure 2 is an illustration of a quad-50 GFT with instructions for its use.

Copies were being made by hand so that each FDC could eventually have one. A paper copy was to be submitted to higher headquarters in Colonel Light's May report.

16 April 1953

The platoon got in another officer today [2nd Lt. Raymond J. Babinsky]. . . . The Battery is now four officers over strength—which cuts out about the last excuse for not letting reserve officers rotate. . . . There are now four officers in our firing platoon alone.

17 April 1953

Having four officers in the platoon really doesn't leave me much to do. . . . I'm here in the hootchie writing this morning while the other three officers are out doing the work. This is too good to last, I'm afraid.

18 April 1953
Dan came to visit to go over career plans once we return to the US.

Our houseboys had picked some wild flowers, put them in jars filled with water, and placed them around the hootchie. Sleeping bags were necessary because the nights were still very cold. Sometime during the evening, as we worked on the maps and a few beers, one of the jars of water holding the flowers was knocked over and spilled into Reimus's sleeping bag. We were unaware that this had happened. Reimus worked late at the FDC and came in about midnight. When he got into his sleeping bag, he found the jar and flowers, and his down liner was soaking wet. He was angry but made the best of the situation. After hanging the wet down-liner over the stove, he rolled up in a blanket inside the sleeping bag cover. After being cold all night, he was sick the next morning with pneumonia-like symptoms. If he had slept in his clothes, with his heavy coat, he would probably have been okay. As it was, it took him several days to recover. I felt very bad about our contribution to his misery, and took his place in the FDC until he was well.

19 April 1953
Still no word. . . . Part of the platoon will start moving back to the airstrip tomorrow. With all the new officers, it's undecided as to who will go. . . . It will take about a week for the move to be completed.

Exchange of Sick and Wounded Prisoners

After resumption of the Panmunjom Peace Talks at the end of March, events moved swiftly. An agreement was reached on 11 April to exchange wounded and sick prisoners—the swap to begin on 20 April. The UN would return 5,800 prisoners, all of whom had received the best medical care and generous food rations. The Americans, on the other hand, were shocked to find that only 149 Americans would be among 684 UN prisoners to be exchanged.

It would soon be learned that 58 percent of American captives had perished in the Communist prison camps (Fehrenbach 1963, 444). The UN wounded received little medical attention—sulfur tablets being the only medicine available. No relief parcels were allowed to be delivered to Communist-held POWs, nor were neutral observers allowed to inspect the camps. UN POWs were fed the ration of a Chinese peasant—a starvation diet for Americans. The prisoners were packed into huts with no toilet

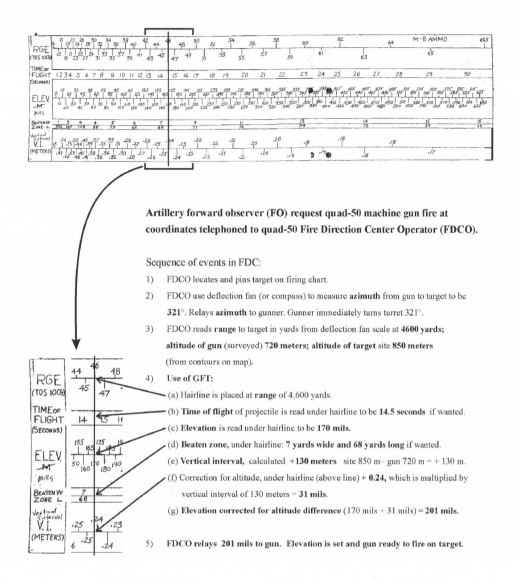

Artillery forward observer (FO) request quad-50 machine gun fire at coordinates telephoned to quad-50 Fire Direction Center Operator (FDCO).

Sequence of events in FDC:

1) FDCO locates and pins target on firing chart.

2) FDCO use deflection fan (or compass) to measure **azimuth** from gun to target to be **321°**. Relays **azimuth** to gunner. Gunner immediately turns turret 321°.

3) FDCO reads **range** to target in yards from deflection fan scale at **4600 yards**; **altitude of gun** (surveyed) **720 meters; altitude of target site 850 meters** (from contours on map).

4) **Use of GFT:**

   (a) Hairline is placed at **range** of 4,600 yards.

   (b) **Time of flight** of projectile is read under hairline to be **14.5 seconds** if wanted.

   (c) **Elevation** is read under hairline to be **170 mils.**

   (d) **Beaten zone,** under hairline: **7 yards wide and 68 yards long** if wanted.

   (e) **Vertical interval,** calculated +**130 meters** site 850 m– gun 720 m = + 130 m.

   (f) Correction for altitude, under hairline (above line) + **0.24,** which is multiplied by vertical interval of 130 meters = **31 mils.**

   (g) **Elevation corrected for altitude difference** (170 mils + 31 mils) = **201 mils.**

5) FDCO relays **201 mils to gun. Elevation is set and gun ready to fire on target.**

FIGURE 2 GRAPHIC FIRING TABLE FOR QUAD-50 (HANDMADE)

Quad-50 position.

Lieutenant Marlow with bunker being built for quad-50 by a Korean Service unit (cost: two packs of cigarettes).

Dan.

Second Lt. Frank C. Malone, Houston, Texas. Dan's replacement, 8 April 1953.

DAN, LIEUTENANT MARLOW, AND LIEUTENANT MALONE

facilities and with only wood fires to combat the sub-zero temperatures. Most of the American prisoners had been captured during the first months of the war. To survive, they had to endure three bitterly cold Korean winters. The wounded died first, then the youngest, then others from starvation and low resistance to disease.

Between 11 April and the exchange on 20 April, the Communists took the opportunity to escalate their aggressiveness, probably to draw public attention away from the fact that 58 percent of the American POWs in their hands had died. For nine miserable days, shelling and attacks took place along the MLR.

The most publicized incident occurred 16 April—a major attack on Pork Chop by two companies of Chinese. A three-day battle ensued during which the enemy occupied Pork Chop. Control of Pork Chop was regained by UN forces, paying a price of several hundred UN casualties. The strategic value of this battle, other than psychological, was questionable at a time when the war was winding down. Up and down the front, the Communists stepped up the shelling of frontline positions, and enemy contacts greatly increased in frequency.

20 April 1953

As usual, in our forward positions, we were not kept abreast of the higher level maneuvers or of enemy action farther down the line. Shortly after the prisoner exchange was announced, Whitlock called for an early afternoon meeting of the company officers.

My new driver, Corporal Benson, was notified to take me there immediately after lunch. Of the several drivers who worked for me in Korea, he was the least talkative. Corporal Benson had come from a farm in the hills of Arkansas and was drafted into the army after dropping out of school. He never spoke except when spoken to, and answered inquiries with a country drawl. After lunch he picked me up for the drive to the company CP.

We drove south along the Mundung-ni Valley, eventually reaching the wide section of the valley where the heaviest concentration of field artillery was located. Amid the forest of cannon barrels were many squad bunkers, CPs, and parked trucks, jeeps, and other vehicles. A line of telephone poles, heavy with communication wires, ran alongside the dusty gravel road.

As we poked along at 20 miles per hour, I saw a puff of black smoke on the hillside 100 yards to my right, about 25 yards from the ground. A cloud of dust was kicked up in a 30-yard circle under the smoke. I couldn't believe my eyes. It looked like an air burst from an artillery shell. While I stared at the spot, another puff of black smoke appeared closer to us, again followed by kicked-up dust underneath. It *was* an air burst. The artillery complex was coming under attack from the enemy using proximity fuse projectiles. The spacing between the air explosion and the ground would indicate the fuses were radar-activated, like our VT (variable timing) fuses. As the Chinese were not supposed to have VT fuses, we wondered whether they were Russian or whether they had been captured from us earlier in the war. A third puff of black smoke was even closer.

"Corporal Benson, speed up! Get the hell out of here as fast as you can!"

"Sir, I have orders to not go faster than 20 miles per hour."

"Dammit, Corporal Benson, floorboard the gas—we're being shelled—I'll take responsibility." He still hesitated.

"Get going or let me drive!" He finally got the message and began to speed up.

"Faster," I shouted, "faster!"

In a few moments we came to the end of the valley, where the road turned behind a cliff, out of sight of the valley. We drove the final mile to the company CP at 20 miles per hour without incident.

The meeting with Whitlock and the other officers lasted about two hours; then we sat around and talked awhile. The main topic was replacement personnel. With the pending end of the fighting, rotation had been sped up. We were losing key people and getting new recruits faster than we could train them. No one complained too much however, since we knew that as reservists the fast train home would be offered to us soon. Whitlock and Nutting were regular army (career officers) and had little interest in cutting short their time in combat. Their future in the army would be determined to a great extent by their time as troop commanders in combat. Whitlock had not even made captain at that time, yet I felt sure he would make field grade before he retired, probably full colonel. I felt he was a good officer, even though we didn't always agree.

In the late afternoon, we started back to our unit. As we approached the valley where the air bursts had caused us to exceed the speed limit, we found the road blocked by a line of jeeps and trucks. The MPs (military police) had put up a roadblock and were letting only one vehicle at a time enter the valley. When our turn came, we followed the road around the cliff.

"Oh my God!" Corporal Benson exclaimed, shocked out of his silence. Before us, all the way down the valley, was a scene of devastation. The air bursts we had seen must have been the registration for the real bombardment. There is little doubt in my mind that the Communists had an infiltrator directing the action.

We knew the enemy had as much artillery as we did, but they almost always conserved their ammunition. Not this time. After we had left the valley at high speed, the Chinese artillery fired a TOT, with hundreds of shells dropping into the valley at the same time, followed by two hours of continuous shelling. Almost everything above ground had been hit. The telephone wires were hanging to the ground rather than strung between the poles. One pole had even been shot off, with the upper part caught in the fallen wires. The road was pitted with shell holes. Nearly every vehicle out in the open had shrapnel holes in its body. An ambulance was riddled with shrapnel and skewed sideways off the road. Nothing was spared. The bombardment included high-explosive rounds as well as the air bursts. Smoke was still rising from smouldering fires. We had been fortunate to get out of the valley before the initial hailstorm of shells dropped in, and I couldn't help think what our fate would have been if we had dillydallied longer.

The 158th and the 189th Field Artillery Battalions were the principal units in the valley, but the 1st Platoon of B Battery from our quad-50 battalion, along with one attached quad-50 halftrack from my platoon, was there in air defense. The AAA quad-50s were dug into the hills around the valley and had suffered little damage. Most of the artillery guns were still able to fire since they were in strong sandbag fortifications, and some were actually returning fire.

We picked our way through the destruction for about one and a half miles before leaving it behind. One mile further up the road, the northern batteries of the 158th Field Artillery Battalion, with which we lived, had hardly been scratched. The constant threat of a rain of shells from the sky kept us on our toes. It was difficult to completely relax as long as you were within firing range.

21 April 1953
Nothing has come out on early release. . . . Tonight I'm going over to visit Dan.

22 April 1953

Baker was pulled into the battery headquarters to take over the executive officer's job, and I am platoon leader again. Half of the platoon halftracks have been changed with those of the 2nd Platoon at the airstrip, but further change is being delayed for a few days. . . . Up here it's not bad, as I have Lieutenant Reimus and Lieutenant Babinsky to do most of the work. . . .

Last night was Aggie Muster Day. I visited Dan and we went to a movie. Later we talked oil deals. . . .

Lieutenant Nutting is leaving tomorrow, being transferred to Japan for a tour of duty there. I'm going in tonight for his going-away party.

The weather over here is much warmer, and the hills are covered with purple flowers that look like baby orchids.

On 11 April 2nd Lt. Stephen F. Flaherty was assigned to A Battery, followed by 2nd Lt. Raymond J. Babinsky on 18 April. C Battery received 2nd Lt. Frank C. Malone on 8 April and 1st Lt. Carl R. Brooks on 27 April. Malone was to be Dan's replacement.

Changing of the Guard

Since Lieutenant Nutting was scheduled to rotate to Japan on 23 April and several NCOs in the company were leaving at the same time to return to the States, Lieutenant Whitlock planned a send-off party at A Battery headquarters for all off-duty personnel for the evening of 22 April. Actually, there were to be two parties: one for the noncoms, and one for the officers. Off-duty people in our platoon headquarters would travel together in one truck. Baker had moved to battery headquarters a few days before, so as the new platoon leader I rode in the cab with the driver. Finch manned the FDC, enabling Reimus to attend the party. Whitlock had an ample supply of scotch available for the officers in his hootchie, along with some nuts and cheese. The enlisted men were served in the NCO mess, with beer and other booze furnished by the sergeants.

The party grew lively, with the men mostly rehashing humorous incidents of the past few months. There was an attempt to sing college songs, with Hamp leading. After an hour or so, I was in need of bladder relief. Lieutenant Whitlock insisted that everyone use the latrine, which was about 50 feet behind the hootchie. With no snow, the night was pitch black. Groping along the trail into the darkness, I stumbled into a foxhole. Shook up, I angrily relieved myself and returned to the party, scratched up and dirty. Whitlock gave me a questionable look, but I said nothing except to complain about the foxhole location. Later another officer left to find his way to the latrine and fell into the same foxhole. He came back scratched up, muddier than I was, and smelling slightly of urine. I tried to look as innocent as possible despite Whitlock's accusing stare. I slept all the way back to our area and was helped up the steps to the officers' hootchie by one of the departing sergeants. Too much free scotch.

23 April 1953

It's a fair warm day here in Korea, but my mind is thousands of miles away with you.

The next morning at dawn, the communications sergeant woke me to say that Lieutenant Whitlock was on the way to pick me up for an inspection of the front. By the time I had my boots and flak jacket on, he was there. His driver took us straight to the most forward gun. We inspected the squad and equipment. Whitlock insisted that we walk the trenches to the other direct fire guns. We climbed into the nearest trench, then began to follow it to the next gun position. We had to get out of the trench and climb about a hundred yards to the top of a ridge to the gun emplacement, then back down to the trench. Portions of the trenches were exposed to sniper fire, requiring us to crouch below the trench rim as we moved along. The trenches went up and down the steep terrain, and soon we were sweating and breathing hard. Whitlock seemed disappointed that I was not more hungover. He stepped up the pace. Again I made no complaint and showed no sign of the activities of the night before, instead chatting normally with him. There was not much firing, although an occasional exploding mortar round could be heard down the line along with some rumbling of outgoing rounds overhead. After two hours Lieutenant Whitlock gave up and had the driver take us back. Those morning walks with the field artillery had paid off. He never mentioned my conduct at the party.

24 April 1953

The 45th Division policy has come down on my category for rotation. If I can meet the qualifications (and I think I can), then the order states that I will leave for home not later than 31 May (thirty-six days away). To apply I must furnish a copy of the original order that directed me to report for active duty. My official 201 file is stored in Chunchon with such an order in it. However, my personal

201 file was left with you. Please search through it for the order, which is dated 27 August 1951, and send me three copies.

Don't get your hopes too high, but right now it looks pretty good.

25 April 1953

I talked with the battalion S-1 [first sergeant] today, and he said I would be leaving for home before the end of May. . . . I still need two copies of the original order putting us on active duty (one for Dan). The S-1 said he would send to the rear for them. . . . I must furnish them within two weeks.

26 April 1953

Today is Sunday so I went to chapel and later to the movies. My main thoughts are of coming home. Lieutenant Baker and Lieutenant Davis are scheduled to leave within ten days. Dan and I should leave on the last shipment of the month. The only thing holding us up is getting copies of the orders that put us on active duty."

27 April 1953

Operation Little Switch, the exchange of sick and wounded, was completed by 26 April. It was anticipated that a final truce would quickly follow. Contrary to expectations, however, the firing did not let up but actually increased during the next three months, until the armistice was signed on 27 July 1953.

28 April 1953

It's warm and raining today—the first time in a month—and things were getting dusty. Everybody seems to be in high spirits over just little things like a change in the weather.

The rain cuts down visibility so much that we can't see the Chinks' lines and they can't see ours. All shooting has just about ceased. It promises to be a lazy, peaceful day.

I'm still patiently waiting for my orders.

30 April 1953

It rained for two days, but now the sun is out and the mud is drying fast. Today is payday and I'll be paid as a first lieutenant. I won't send any of the money home in view of my pending departure.

This afternoon I'm going into the battalion for a class. At that time I will submit my letter, as I believe the awaited orders have come up from the rear.

1 May 1953

Yesterday I turned in my letter and was told that I would probably leave here on 26 May. The exact date isn't definite yet. I'll leave from Inchon by ship probably within four days after I leave my unit. The ship will make a four-day cruise to Sasebo, where we will pick up our baggage stored there. After a fourteen-days sailing we'll dock in San Francisco. From there we'll travel to the fort nearest our home, probably Fort Sam Houston in San Antonio.

Well, I've got to get to work—the thought of you is constantly on my mind.

2 May 1953

It's a fair day here. I'm taking it easy just loafing here in the hootchie. . . . Lieutenant Reimus and I are the only two officers in our platoon now. He works the FDC and I take care of the tracks.

The battalion was now some 30 percent over strength, a far cry from when I had arrived in December. Dan was offered R&R in Japan but turned it down in hopes to rotate earlier. The daily routine went on as before. More artillery fire—both friendly and enemy—took place in May, June, and July 1953 than in any other months during the war. At Panmunjom the Communists had not agreed to the UN truce proposals. Savage fighting broke out in spots along the front to put pressure on the UN. A certain uneasiness began to affect my thinking, especially when shells exploded close by. I only had a few days to go until I could return home to my wife. Like my doctor friend, I felt more comfortable inside the bunkers.

4 May 1953

I've missed writing the last couple of days, getting ready for a command inspection. Today the inspection came off well—that should be the last one I'll have to stand.

Replacements are coming in by the hundreds. The whole battery has changed in the last two months. . . . There is a good show on tonight, Rainbow Around My Shoulder. *I'm in good spirits and the movie will just top it off. . . .*

Here we ride a rattling jeep over a dusty rocky road with no lights and slowly freeze since we have to leave the windshield off. You'd be surprised just how much a pleasure it will be to be able to drive with headlights, have a windshield to knock off the wind, and best of all to have pavement under the wheels.

6 May 1953

Baker and Davis already have their orders, and indications are that we'll get out right on time. I'm going to take it as easy as I can and still do my job. It's getting too near rotation to take any unnecessary chances.

8 May 1953

Davis and Baker had orders to leave on the 7th but the ship was late, and they are now leaving on the 13th. It's rainy and cold today. . . . Dan and I are going to get together at noon. Received your Easter box and really enjoyed it.

9 May 1953

I'm moving my tracks back into antiaircraft defense positions around the field artillery [but I am to remain in my present bachelor officers' quarters until I rotate, to help with the indirect firing]. . . . Everyone is packing and getting ready to leave, it seems. Baker and Davis are leaving Tuesday along with a good many sergeants and other enlisted men. I will be leaving in two weeks, so I'm packing my duffel bag too. . . .

What these last few letters fail to say, I will tell you in person.

10 May 1953

It's a cool cloudy Sunday morning. . . . Today we're changing our winter clothes for summer dress, and our heavy sleeping bags for thin ones. Even so, it's cold enough to wear a coat.

13 May 1953

Baker and Davis have left and I'm next on the list. Only thirteen more days—or so. As they say over here, 12 more get-up's and a get-up and go!

I've been getting the platoon in order for Lieutenant Reimus to take over. . . . Now that I'm on the tracks instead of the FDC, I'm making my last contribution to the army by improving the firing technique. We've made a few steps lately, for which I'm quite proud. These heavy machine guns have been developed into a very efficient and dependable indirect fire weapon.

14 May 1953

Today is cold and rainy again. I've been out looking over the track positions and found a spot that I believe will give us the best field of fire of any in the battery.

I plan to get the engineers to start working on the road up to it right away. I plan to bury myself in work for the next twelve days so that time will pass more quickly. The battery commander offered me the battery executive job, but I have such a short time to go, I turned it down.

15 May 1953

Today my jeep has been broken down most of the day, so I haven't been able to get around and do much. The weather has been rainy and cool.

16 May 1953

This morning I had to get up early to go out to one of the tracks. I thought about how nice it will be to drive along a smooth Texas highway with the windows down.

17 May 1953

Last night word came down that Dan and I will leave on the 21st of May—Thursday—only four days away. When you receive this letter I will probably be on the ship on my way home.

18 May 1953

On 17 May, both Dan and I received orders to depart on 21 May. Lieutenant Whitlock asked me to come to A Battery headquarters to complete my records before departing. He was very complimentary of my tour, and I told him that I was proud to have served in his command. He said that he had recommended me for a Bronze Star (it was granted 9 June 1953, while I was aboard ship). At the time I could have cared less—I just wanted to go home. Whitlock said there was one charge that had to be cleared up before I could leave:

"You still owe twenty-five dollars for the gunner's quadrant."

"Dammit Whit, that was stolen by the ROKs. You sent us up that hill that night, with the driver arguing it was impassable. It was my second day in combat. I didn't know what was going on. Can't you show it as lost in battle?"

He had touched a sore spot with me. It seemed foolish that I would make an issue of this when it could delay my departure. He finally dropped the subject. Years later I learned he had paid the $25 out of his own pocket.

19 May 1953

Lieutenant Colonel Light began to include a summary of the fire missions in his monthly report to higher headquarters. Typical of these is his report of May 1953:

> This battalion [145th AAA AW] fired 734,316 rounds of caliber .50 ammunition during the period. On 5 May the 5,000,000th round in combat in Korea was fired. Results of the fire during May show an estimated sixty-four enemy killed and an estimated forty wounded. In addition, groups of enemy were dispersed twenty-nine times, eighteen enemy machine guns were silenced, six snipers were silenced, and three loudspeakers were forced to discontinue operations. . . . More than 79 tons of caliber .50 brass was turned into ordnance. (145th AAA AW Battalion Reports)

Our 145th AAA AW Battalion had fired 734,316 rounds of 50-caliber in May, the greatest quantity for any month since it had been in combat. The month of May was the battalion's seventeenth month on the front lines. During that time the battalion had fired five and a half million rounds of 50-caliber ammunition, more than half of which (about three million rounds) was fired in the last five months, i.e., January through May of 1953. My platoon and Dan's had fired more than our share.

20 May 1953 (1:20 AM)

It's early in the morning here in Korea. . . . I'm in the FDC, where I'm staying up all night. This is my last night near the front and I don't want to go to bed—especially since last night we got shelled so badly I couldn't sleep.

Early tomorrow morning I will take the jeep to the rear and leave the Korean front for good. It's a good feeling. Here in the FDC the night is quiet, and we have the radio playing soft, sexy music—rotation music we call it. I'm just sleepy enough to feel light-headed, and you are constantly on my mind.

A great sense of caution came over me. After making one round of the gun positions to tell everyone goodbye, I stayed close to my hootchie. On 20 May, my last night, I packed all my gear into my duffel bag, rolled my sleeping bag, and spent the night in the strongly fortified FDC.

As second lieutenants, Smoke Valley, December 1952.

At Heartbreak Ridge five months later as first lieutenants, May 1953.

45th Division Records Company.

Civilian huts.

The backyard.

Rice paddies.

CHUNCHON, MAY 1953

Leaving Korea

21 May 1953 (Chunchon)

We've already completed the first leg of our trip home. Dan, Lieutenant Marlow, and I left bag and baggage this morning and are about 50 miles to the rear at Chunchon [the 45th Division Records Company]. Here we will get our records straight. We're now loafing until Saturday morning, when we'll take the train to Inchon. Then we should catch a ship leaving directly for the States on the night of 25 May (Monday). . . .

It feels good to be out of range of enemy guns and on our way home. . . .

P.S. Don't send my uniform to California—I'm not sure we'll land there. Anyway, they will issue us a suit of khakis to come home in.

Second letter, late evening, 21 May:

It's late evening here in Chunchon. We've had a busy day getting our records in order and preparing to leave. This portion of Korea is densely populated. Due to the heavy fighting that took place here at one time, all of the larger buildings and most homes have been destroyed. Many people live in shacks and huts of mud and straw. As in most of the Orient, sewerage consists of a gutter in front of the row of huts, and a stream in back to furnish water. Rice paddies, which cover the countryside, are just showing green sprouts above the water. Human waste, used as fertilizer, smells up the whole area.

The people, though, are very robust—the kids are rosy-cheeked, always running and laughing. They wear funny little rubber shoes, like slippers, that are turned up at the toes. When they come to a stream (the whole country is cut up with swift mountain streams), they never think about looking for a bridge. They just slosh right on across as though it weren't there. The streams are lined with women squatting down by the edge and beating their clothes clean on a rock.

The straw roofs make the countryside look as though it were dotted with haystacks. The people sleep on the warm floor rather than heat up the whole interior of the hut. . . .

"We will loaf here tomorrow at the replacement center but take the train early Saturday for Inchon. . . . Two ships sail for the West Coast—either San Francisco or Seattle for a fourteen-day trip—but one sails for New York, a thirty-four day trip through Honolulu and the Panama Canal—ugh. . . . I'll write you in Inchon.

22 May 1953 (Chunchon)

Today we're still loafing around killing time. Nothing new.

24 May 1953 (Inchon)

We're in a rotation BOQ here at Inchon after taking an all-day train ride from Chunchon yesterday.

This morning we went through a mountain of paperwork and forms. It is indefinite whether we will go to Seattle or San Francisco; it's also uncertain how our discharge will be handled. We were warned not to have anyone meet us because of the uncertainty. We will probably have to take a troop train to our point of discharge.

I'm satisfied with the fact that we are making progress.

We turned in our combat equipment and uniforms. In return we received our duffel bags with the summer-weight clothes from the States, which had been kept in storage for us, as well as those from Sasebo. The army had realized that it was too costly to stop in Japan just to pick up luggage. We had a naked feeling giving up our carbine, pistol, steel helmet, and flak jacket. We completed our processing through the Inchon Replacement Depot and were issued a slip giving us clearance to leave Korea.

We were taken by bus to the port and put in barracks to await our troop ship. My bunk was in a room with about twenty other officers, most of whom were returning from combat areas. We had an excellent officers' mess with types of food we had not had for months. Best of all, we had access to an officers' club built on a rocky knoll overlooking Inchon Bay. It had been built by the Japanese when they occupied Korea. It was very elaborate, with glass walls and polished wood paneling. We could sit under trimmed shade trees, in sculptured rock gardens, and drink beer while viewing the blue waters of the bay. We didn't have to worry about incoming rounds.

25 May 1953 (Inchon)

The officers in my BOQ were in bed asleep when an air-raid siren began to wail with deafening volume outside our barracks. A noncom came running down the aisle, screaming, "Air raid! Air raid! Get to the air raid shelter!"

No one moved. We had heard about "bed check Charlie," a small, single-engine, propellor-driven biplane that sometimes circled over Seoul and Inchon at night, hand-dropping a few small bombs. We could hear the far off sputter of a small engine. After surviving artillery and mortar bombardments nightly for months, the thought of danger from this small plane was laughable.

The noncom became frantic: "Get up you guys, you've got to get to the air raid shelter!"

No one moved.

"Alright, it's your own fault if you get killed." He ran out.

From the dark someone said: "That rear echelon bastard thinks this is an air raid."

There was a faint sound of an explosion miles away. Everyone went back to sleep.

27 May 1953 (Inchon)

We've moved to a different set of barracks here at Inchon. We have completed all the processing and are "waiting for our ship to come in." I'm reading one novel after another. It feels good to have no one except yourself to take care of—no responsibility at all.

If all goes according to schedule, we'll load ship on the 29th of May and arrive in San Francisco (or Seattle) around the 12th or 13th of June. Then we will probably take a troop train somewhere for separation. . . . We can only wait and see. I tried shopping but everything here has been picked over.

(This was the last letter written to Robbie during my tour of duty.)

28 May 1953 (Leaving Korea)

As of 28 May 1953 I had been in Korea for five months—161 days to be exact. At a glance this seems a relatively short time. However, 146 of these days had been in the combat zone, with only a 15-day break in tents at the airstrip during the entire period. The other 131 days I was "in harm's way," living in bunkers constantly exposed to enemy fire. Mortar and artillery fire fell into our platoon area daily. I did not feel that I was "bugging out," and I was glad to be leaving.

On 28 May, we were loaded on a landing craft and taken out to the troop ship. The ship, the USS *General Black,* embarked that night. Officers were assigned four to a stateroom, while enlisted men were in rows of five-tier bunks in the hole. Everyone was given a job to do while aboard ship. I was made commander of stairwell #3, with a crew of about ten enlisted men. We had to clean and scrub the stairwell each morning, then stand by for inspection. We still had plenty of time off. There were movies every night.

We were fed four meals per day so that we would look good when we arrived home. I had lost about twenty pounds during my tour and was in good shape.

About the third day at sea, we ran into a major storm. For days the ship pitched through big waves, accompanied by rain and high winds. Many

Dudley at Inchon Bay Officers' Club.

View from Inchon Bay Officers' Club.

LST to troop ship.

*Dan and three other officers aboard
USS General Black.*

DEPARTING KOREA, MAY 1953

got seasick. Even though I didn't get sick, an uneasy lump developed in my stomach so that I lost interest in eating. The fourteen-day crossing seemed much longer.

On 10 June we passed under the Golden Gate Bridge and docked in San Francisco. There was a military band playing and many wives and family waiting and cheering on the dock. I had asked Robbie to wait and meet me in San Antonio, as I was scheduled to take a train to Fort Sam Houston from San Francisco. Not everyone felt that way. One sergeant had written his wife: "When we land in San Francisco, I'm going to catch up on my screwing. You'd better be there if you want to get in on it."

We checked into the BOQ at Fort Mason, California. I called Robbie and talked to her for the first time since November 1952. She cried and blubbered. Both of us could hardly wait to meet in San Antonio. Sometimes I think we were too practical.

A group of us took in the town and greatly enjoyed the restaurants and bars of San Francisco. What a relief to be back in the United States.

On 14 June we boarded the train for San Antonio. Two men were assigned to each small compartment. Dan and I were roommates again. The train traveled to Los Angeles, where we switched to another line to take the southern route to Texas. It was desert most of the way. We read, ate, and spent the evenings at the bar. Three days later, on the seventeenth, we arrived at Fort Sam Houston in San Antonio. Soon we began processing for separation, which primarily consisted of a physical examination by a group of doctors. I had some loss of hearing, probably because in all the firing we never wore earplugs. Then we were each granted five days of leave.

Robbie arrived. She was even more beautiful than I had remembered. As we embraced, I told her we had five days leave, all to ourselves—another honeymoon—but no fishing! No fishing, she agreed!

On 24 June 1953, I was released from active duty.

The Korean Miracle

My brother, Dan, visited Japan and South Korea in the 1980s and was astounded to find that both Tokyo and Seoul were bustling modern cities with skyscrapers—a far cry from the destroyed cities we remembered. By the turn of the century, both countries were world-class business powers with standards of living almost equal to that of the United States. I have often wondered whether my brilliant houseboy, Gene, and Lieutenant Lee

USS General Black *troop transport.*

Storm at sea.

Golden Gate Bridge, San Francisco.

*When the fat lady sings, it's over
(San Francisco welcome).*

THE TRIP HOME, JUNE 1953

were leaders in the new Korean miracle. Certainly, South Koreans' close association with American servicemen during the war and the years following has had a great influence on their country's development.

After fifty years North Korea, by comparison, is still a backward, poverty-stricken country that has become in effect a Stalinist prison for its citizens. Its leader, Kim Jong Il, maintains a million-man "goose stepping" army, reminiscent of Hitler's, which keeps the country's treasury drained. Its "rulers are indifferent to the mass starvation of their own people—one whose citizens are, on average, more than seven inches shorter than their Southern brothers and sisters, and one that requires its citizens to rise early in the morning to join screeching public-address systems in singing absurd songs of praise to a deranged leader . . . Kim Johg Il is both evil and lunatic 'and doomed.' . . . The regime's threats against other countries is evidence of its isolation, desperation and declining hold on power" (WSJ, 2003).

Whereas, the Communist governments of Russia and its eastern satellite countries have collapsed, and China is moderating its stance on Communism, Pyongyang, the capital of North Korea, still exists as in the days of the Cold War. Surely intelligent people in North Korea and the remaining Communist countries in the world must realize the futility of their Communist philosophies.

The success of South Korea gives me a deep sense of satisfaction and makes me feel that my participation in the Korean War was worthwhile. I feel pride in having served in a combat situation where freedom has been preserved for a nation of people (see figure 3).

The Aftermath

One month after I was released from active duty, the Korean War fighting ended with the signing of the armistice on 27 July 1953. By that time I was working as a petroleum geologist for the oil subsidiary of United Gas Company, in Jackson, Mississippi. Robbie and I were buying a small new house using the GI Bill for financing. The war already seemed an obscure incident in my past as I concentrated on my new job, which I was enjoying very much.

After being released from active duty I was still not free from the military. All able-bodied men had to serve a total of eight years, either on active duty, in the Reserves, or in the National Guard. My active-duty time and National Guard time counted, but I still had five years to go. The only

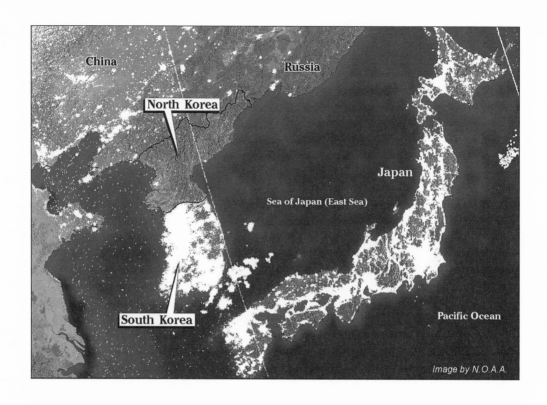

FIGURE 3 SATELLITE VIEW OF KOREA AND JAPAN, FIFTY YEARS AFTER
THE WAR. PROSPEROUS SOUTH KOREA AWASH WITH LIGHT WHILE
COMMUNIST NORTH KOREA IS STILL IN THE "DARK AGES."

Army Reserve Unit in Jackson was Military Government, so my quad-50 experience fell by the wayside. During my five years in the Reserves, I made weekly meetings, went to two-week summer camps, and eventually was promoted to captain. But military government was so boring that I resigned my officer's commission when the five years was up.

About ten years after being released from active duty, a Christmas card informed me that Lieutenant Whitlock was assigned to Command and General Staff School at Fort Leavenworth, Kansas. I took the opportunity to visit him there. He had been promoted to major and was friendly but had developed a rather stiff formal military attitude. Possibly he still remembered the gunner's quadrant. More likely, being under intense scrutiny, he may have been afraid I would embarrass him if I became unruly.

On a summer vacation in about 1965, Robbie and I were driving through Georgia with our two daughters of grammar-school age. In Moultrie we visited Hamp Davis, who owned the gas distribution system serving the town. He was newly married to a pretty Georgia girl. We spent the night with them and barbequed in his backyard. Hamp and I reminisced over our Korean experiences into the early hours of the morning and got so drunk that our wives wouldn't speak to us the next morning.

For many years I gave little thought to my Korean experiences. However, when the fiftieth anniversary of the Korean War was imminent, my interest revived. I have read many different books on the war, but all were about the first year of fighting with a bare mention of the two years of trench warfare that followed. A new book by James Brady, *The Coldest War,* really captured my attention, as he was in the marines stationed in the high mountains immediately east of our Smoke Valley area. He wrote about his tour in the frontline trenches, which lasted from November 1951 to July 1952 (nine months, thirty-six points), and described the same war that I remembered. By the time I arrived in Korea (December 1952), his sector had been taken over by the ROKs. The thought occurred to me that if his experiences were worth writing about, perhaps mine were too.

All of the characters mentioned in this account are real, but in most cases only the actual names of the officers were used, as they were repeatedly mentioned in the battalion reports. Names of many of the enlisted men have escaped my memory after fifty years.

Colonel Light's report for May 1953, dated 6 June 1953, included a recommendation "that consideration be given to publishing appropriate directives on the tactics and techniques of indirect fire with the M-16 multiple machine gun (quad-50), and that a special authorization to augment the current TO&E be granted to provide necessary FDC personnel and equipment when an indirect fire role is being performed." He included with the report a proposed standing operating procedure (SOP) in great detail for indirect fire with the quad-50s, dated 9 May 1953. Also included in the report was a drawing of his graphic firing table (GFT slide rule) designed for FDC use to greatly speed up calculations for settings for the guns. Attached to the report were supporting statements from Maj. Gen. P. D. Ginder, commanding general of the 45th Division, and Col. Harold E. Marr Jr., commander of 45th Division Artillery, among others.

William Donnelly, the army historian at Fort McNair, informed me that the M-16 quad-50s were rendered obsolete after the Korean War, and the recommendations of Colonel Light were not approved. Instead, the quad-50s were given to National Guard units and eventually discarded. I was very disappointed to learn this, as they had been proven to be an exceptionally useful weapon in Korea.

Dan and I formed our own oil company in 1960 and were quite successful. He operated our company's western division out of Beeville, Texas, while I ran the eastern division out of Jackson, Mississippi. After twenty years of operation, we had offices in Calgary, London, and Perth, Australia. In recent years we have sold most of our assets and are now partially retired.

Robbie and I celebrated our fiftieth wedding anniversary in 2001. She still likes to fish, but now it's Atlantic salmon in Canada. She is still "raking in the money," but now by investing in the stock market.

Appendix: Units of the US Tenth (X) Corps

March 1953, in Addition to the US 45th and 40th Divisions

5th Regimental Combat Team

The historical core of the 5th Regimental Combat Team (RCT) was the 5th Infantry Regiment, the third oldest regiment in the US Army, dating back before 1812. A regimental combat team is essentially a reinforced infantry regiment organized to operate independently, with an attached artillery battalion, armor, and engineer elements, generally about 3,500 men. The 5th RCT consisted of three infantry battalions including a tank company and heavy mortar company, the 555th Field Artillery Battalion, the 72nd Engineering Company, a service company, and a medical company.

On 1 January 1949, the US Army's 5th RCT, made up of components of larger units being moved out, was reactivated in Seoul for occupation duty in South Korea. It was the last Army combat unit to leave South Korea before the North Korean invasion.

In June 1949 the 5th RCT was transported by ship from Inchon, Korea, to Honolulu, where it was housed in the Schofield Barracks. The Korean War began one year later on 25 June 1950. The 5th RCT was shipped back to Korea, debarking at Pusan on 1 August 1950, to reinforce the three US Army divisions that had been rushed over from Japan. These outnumbered forces suffered many casualties during those first months.

Except for a short period guarding prisoners on Kŏje-do Island, Korea, the 5th RCT remained in combat during the entire Korean war. It was occupying the Punchbowl, attached to the 45th Division, when the Korean War ended.

ROK 7th Division

The ROK 7th Division was one of the early Republic of Korea divisions and was deployed along the 38th parallel on 25 June 1950 when the North Koreans invaded the South. They were involved in many battles and suffered numerous casualties over the three years of war. The unit was assigned to the X Corps by 1 July 1951.

ROK 12th Division

The ROK 12th Division, newly activated (infantry), was assigned to the US X Corps and deployed along the US 45th Division front line in late December 1952, replacing US infantry.

ROK 20th Division

On 9 February 1953 the ROK 20th Division (infantry) was assigned to the X Corps and to the front lines of the US 5th RCT in the Punchbowl, replacing the 5th RCT infantry.

Glossary of Terms and Abbreviations

AAA AW   army antiaircraft artillery automatic weapons

AAA   army antiaircraft artillery

Aggie   Texas A&M alumnus

API   armor-piercing incendiary

BC   battery commander

bird colonel   full colonel

BOQ   bachelor officers' quarters

CBR   chemical, biological, and radiological

CP   command post

EUSAK   8th US Army of Korea

FA   field artillery

FDC   fire direction center

FO   forward observer

GFT   graphic firing table

GST   graphic site table

hootchie   bunker

KATUSA   Korean augmentation to the US Army

light colonel   lieutenant colonel

MLR   main line of resistance

MP   military police

NCO   noncommissioned officer

POW   prisoner of war

PX   post exchange

quad-50s   four 50-caliber machine guns mounted on a turret

R&R   rest and relaxation leave

RCT   regimental combat team

ROK   Republic of Korea

ROTC   Reserve Officers' Training Corps

S-1   officer in charge of personnel

S-2   officer in charge of intelligence

S-3   officer in charge of operations

S-4   officer in charge of ordnance

TO&E   table of organization and equipment

TOT   time on target

USO   United Service Organizations

References

145th AAA AW Battalion Reports. Declassified archives. College Park, Md., January–May 1953.

Alexander, Bevin. *Korea: The First War We Lost.* New York: Hippocrene Books, 1986.

Brady, James. *The Coldest War: A Memoir of Korea.* New York: Orion Books, 1990.

———. *The Marines of Autumn: A Novel of the Korean War.* New York: Thomas Dunne Books, St. Martin's Press, 2000.

Carroll, Andrew, ed. *War Letters: Extraordinary Correspondence from American Wars.* New York: Scribner, 2001.

Fehrenbach, T. R. *This Kind of War: The Classic Korean War History.* Washington, D.C.: Brassey's, 1963.

Goulden, Joseph C. *Korea: The Untold Story of the War.* New York: McGraw-Hill, 1982.

Hastings, Max. *The Korean War.* New York: Simon and Schuster, 1987.

Hermes, Walter G. *Truce Tent and Fighting Front.* Washington, D.C.: Office of the Chief of Military History, United States Army (for sale by the Superintendent of Documents, U.S. Government Printing Office, CMH Pub. 20-3-1), 1966.

Hickey, Michael. *The Korean War: The West Confronts Communism.* Woodstock, N.Y.: Overlook Press, 2000.

Hogg, Ian V., and John S. Weeks. *Military Small Arms of the 20th Century.* Iola, Wisc.: Krause Publications, 2000.

Office of Chief of Military History. "Historic Survey of Direct Fire Weapons in World War II and the Korean War: A Compendium in Support of the Ardfire Study Group." Historic manuscript file, College Park, Md., 1963.

Pruitt, Frank O. *Reminiscence of a Forgotten War: The Memoirs of Frank O. Pruitt of His Korean War Service with the 40th Division, 1952–1953.* Lake Charles, La.: F. O. Pruitt, 1999.

———. *Delayed Letters from Korea: Thirty-Five Korean War Veterans Reveal Their Unique Stories of America's Least Known War.* Bloomington, Ind.: 1st Books Library, 2002.

Slater, Michael. *Hills of Sacrifice: The 5th RCT in Korea.* Paducah, Ky.: Turner Publishing Company, 2000.

Toland, John. *In Mortal Combat: Korea, 1950–1953.* New York: William Morrow, 1991.

Tucker, Spencer C., ed. *Encyclopedia of the Korean War: A Political, Social, and Military History.* New York: Checkmark Books, 2002.

[WSJ.] "A Defector's Story." *Wall Street Journal.* June 5, 2003.

Acknowledgments

Thanks are due for the contributions of many who aided me in gathering the fifty-year-old information that made this account of the Korean War accurate and informative. My twin brother, Dan A. Hughes, was in the same unit as I, and attached to the adjacent infantry regiment. He recalled many of the stories and details of actions that I had forgotten and supplied me with most of the pictures used herein. His contributions are responsible for a good portion of this narrative.

Alvin Byrd spent many weeks searching for maps from different sources until he was able to draw the maps used here on his computer as a combination of many bits of information. He also used his computer drafting techniques to arrange the illustrations and pictures from various sources.

Col. James Michael Turner, previously from Mississippi, on active duty in the Pentagon at the time of my writing, offered to help me find records in the military archives. He spent considerable time escorting me to potential sources of information. At Fort McNair, we met with William Donnelly, a military historian, who furnished me a great deal of information regarding the last year of the war and the use of the quad-50 machine guns in infantry combat. He provided me a copy of the US Army military history book, which expanded on the last two years of the Korean War, *Truce Tent and Fighting Front,* by Walter G. Hermes. This proved to be very helpful, as it had descriptions of two of the battles in which I was involved (Hill 854 and Hill 812). He also directed me to the archives at College Park, Maryland, where the monthly reports of the 145th AAA AW Battalion—my old unit—were made available. These included a day-by-day report of the unit's activities and the order of battle, as well as map overlays showing gun positions for each month. It seemed incredible that these fifty-year-old detailed reports were available, just as they had been received from the battlefield. From these sources of information, I was able to compile a very complete report of my tour of duty.

My mother, Winnie Hughes, had kept all the letters my brother and I had written to her while we were in Korea. My wife, Robbie, discovered some 150 letters that I had written to her from Korea. With these letters and all the other information, I was able to present a daily account, actually a diary, of my tour of duty.

Brian Meehl, a professional writer, reviewed the manuscript and offered several suggestions that greatly improved its readability; he also provided me much encouragement. Robert J. Bailey, who had served as a spotter plane pilot in Vietnam, edited the manuscript with particular attention to military correctness. Finally, I owe thanks to my secretary, Ruth Wallace, who contributed a great deal of time and showed extreme patience during the eighteen months I worked on the manuscript.